Index

See Basic Instructions for Cutting, Sewing, Layering, Quilting and Binding on pages 58 - 61.

TIPS: As a Guide for Yardage:
Each 1/4 yard or a 'Fat Quarter' equals 3 strips
A pre-cut 'Jelly Roll' strip is 2½" x 42"
Cut 'Fat Quarter' strips to 2½" x 21"

YARDAGE: Yardage is given for using either fabric yardage or 'Jelly Roll' strips

Tans

Greens

Reds

Browns

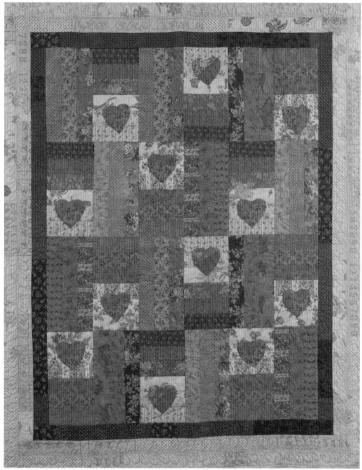

Hearts A Flutter Quilt

SIZE: 48" x 60"

Yardage

We used a *Moda* 'Chelsea' by Blackbird Designs.
'Jelly Roll' collection of pre-cut 2½" fabric strips
- we purchased 1 'Jelly Roll'.

Blocks: ½ yd of Reds OR 5 strips 2½" x 42"
              1 yd of Greens OR 11 strips 2½" x 42"
              ¾ yd of Browns OR 8 strips 2½" x 42"
              1½ yd of Tans OR 16 strips 2½" x 42"

Inner Border   Browns (yardage included above - 5 strips)
Outer Borders Tans (yardage included above - 10 strips)
Binding   Purchase ¼ yd Tans for 6 strips
Hearts   Purchase ¼ yd Reds (3 strips 2½" x 42")
Backing   Purchase 2¾ yds, piece it to 52" x 64"
Batting   Purchase 52" x 64"
Freezer Paper for Applique, Sewing machine, needle, thread

continued on pages 24 - 25

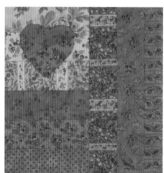

Hearts a Flutter

Hand appliquéd hearts complement the nostalgic feeling in this design. You are going to love the ease with which this project goes together. Simple blocks make Hearts a Flutter great for beginners.

Reds

Browns

Blues

Oranges

Greens

Creams
and
Beiges

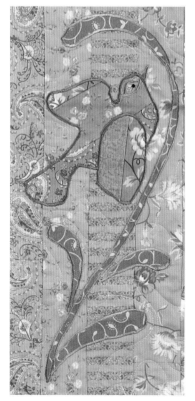

Bluebirds Quilt

SIZE: 34" x 48"

Yardage

We purchased *Moda* 'Folklorique' by Fig Tree
Purchase the following fabrics:

Center of Quilt
¾ yd of Greens (8 strips 2½" x 42")
¾ yd of Oranges (8 strips 2½" x 42")

Inner Border and Bluebirds
½ yd of Blues (3 strips 2½" x 42")

Piano Keys Outer Border
¾ yd of Creams/Beiges (10 strips 2½" x 42")

Binding
Oranges (yardage included above - 5 strips)

Applique
Blues (yardage included above)
¼ yd of Brown (2 strips 2½" x 42")
Purchase 1 yd of Steam A Seam II

Backing   Purchase 1½ yd, piece it to 38" x 52"
Batting   Purchase 38" x 52"
Sewing machine, needle, thread

continued on pages 26 - 29

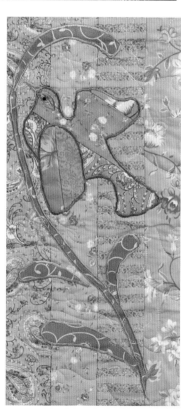

Bluebirds of Happiness

Ever wonder what to do with a handful of strips that are only a yard each?
Bluebirds of Happiness provides a delightful opportunity to use small amounts
of a variety of strips and the fast fuse appliqué makes this quilt fun to make.

Ivory

Yellows

Pinks

Greens

Purples

Reds

**Border
and
Binding**
Green Print

Spring Showers Pillow

SIZE: 16" x 16"

We used leftover strips from *Moda* 'Sanctuary'.

Pillow Top
  ¼ yd Ivory OR 2 strips 2½" x 42"
  ¼ yd Reds OR 2 strips 2½" x 42"
Applique
  1 of each strip 2½" x 21" (Red, Yellow, Purple)
  1 Green strip 2½" x 21"
Backing   Purchase ¾ yd
Purchase Polyfil or Layers of Batting for stuffing
3 *Dritz* 1¼" diameter Buttons to Cover
Extra fabric for Buttons or Yo-Yos

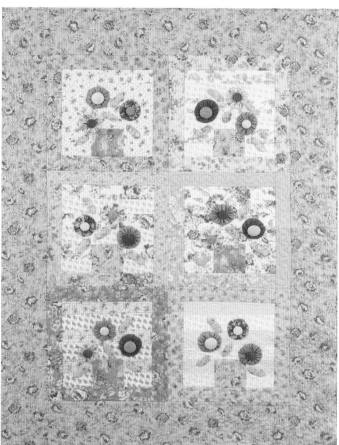

Spring Showers Quilt
by Linda Rocamontes
SIZE: 44" x 60"

Yardage

We used *Moda* 'Sanctuary' by 3 Sisters
'Jelly Roll' collection of pre-cut 2½" fabric strips
- we purchased 1 'Jelly Roll'.

Flower Blocks
  ½ yd of Purples OR 5 strips 2½" x 42"
  1 yd of Ivory OR 11 strips 2½" x 42"
  ½ yd of Yellows OR 6 strips 2½" x 42"
  ½ yd of Greens OR 6 strips 2½" x 42"
  ½ yd of Pinks OR 5 strips 2½" x 42"
Leaf Applique
  Greens (yardage included above - 3 strips)
Gathered Flower Applique
  ¼ yd of Reds (or 2 strips 2½" x 42")
  Yellows (yardage included above - 2 strips)
  Purples (yardage included above - 2 strips)

Border and Binding
  Purchase 1½ yd of Green print
Backing   Purchase 1¼ yds, piece it to 48" x 64"
Batting   Purchase 48" x 64"

Dritz Buttons to Cover
  Six 1⅝" diameter
  Twelve 1¼" diameter
    Note: Do not use buttons on a quilt that will be used
    by babies or toddlers. Substitute Yo-Yo circles.
Sewing machine, needle, thread

continued on pages 32 - 35

Spring Showers

I love fabric covered buttons and yo-yo flowers are so easy to make.
Spring Showers will be a welcome addition to your seasonal décor. Brighten
someone's day with this wonderful gift any time of the year.

Tan prints

Tan Feathers

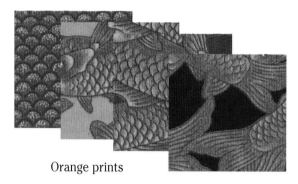

Orange prints

Navy Blue prints

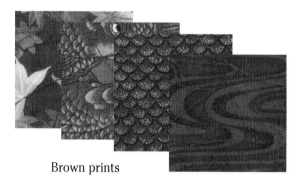

Brown prints

Red/Orange prints

Backside

Black Swirl fabric

Cranes Quilt

SIZE: 54" x 74"

Yardage

We purchased *Moda* 'Koi Garden' by Sentimental Studios collection of fabrics.

Blocks
  Purchase 2¼ yd of Oranges (26 strips 2½" x 42")

First Block Border
  Purchase 1¾ yd Navy Blues (22 strips 2½" x 42")

Second Block Border - Sashing
  Purchase ¾ yd Tans and prints (8 strips 2½" x 42")

Inner Quilt Border and Corners
  Purchase ¾ yd Black marbled (7 strips)

Second Quilt Border
  Oranges (yardage included above - 6 strips)

Outside Quilt Border
  Oranges (yardage included above - 4 strips)
  Navy Blues (yardage included above - 4 strips)

Binding
  Navy Blues (yardage included above - 7 strips)

Applique Cranes
  Black Swirl or Black Marbled (yardage included above)
  ¼ yd of Tan Feather
  ¼ yd of White
  ¼ yd of Red
  Purchase 1¼ yd of Steam A Seam II fusible web

Backing   Purchase 3 yds pieced to 58" x 78"
Batting   Purchase 58" x 78"

continued on pages 36 - 39

Cranes

A common motif in Eastern art, Cranes allows you to express your interest in simple beauty. Constructed in a similar manner as the 'Koi for Good Luck', this quilt takes the design to a higher level with the addition of machine appliqué.

Koi for Good Luck

Adventurous colors make this beautiful quilt a treat to own. Create exciting movement with gorgeous fabrics randomly cut and sewn into strips.

SIZE: 54" x 54"

Yardage

We purchased *Moda* Koi Garden by Sentimental Studios. collection of fabrics, see page 10

Blocks	2½ yd of Red/Oranges (25 strips 2½" x 42")
Block Borders	1¼ yd of Browns (15 strips 2½" x 42")
Sashing	½ yd of Tans (4 strips 2½" x 42")
Sashing Corners	⅛ yd of Black (1 strip 2½" x 42")
Piano Keys Border	Red/Oranges (yardage included above - 8 strips)
	Browns (yardage included above - 8 strips)
Binding:	Red/Oranges ((yardage included above - 6 strips)

Backing
    Purchase 2½ yds, piece it to 58" x 58"
Batting
    Purchase 58" x 58"
Sewing machine, needle, thread

continued on pages 40 - 41

Leaves Table Topper

For those who enjoy smaller projects, this beautiful design is simply elegant with attractive earth tones of color.

SIZE: 22" x 42"

Yardage

We purchased *Moda* Koi Garden by Sentimental Studios.
collection of fabrics, see page 10

Blocks	¾ yd of 6 Red/Oranges (9 strips 2½" x 42")
Block Borders	½ yd of Browns (4 strips 2½" x 42")
Corners	⅛ yd of Black (1 strip 2½" x 42")
Sashing Strips	½ yd of Tans (4 strips 2½" x 42")
Binding:	Red/Oranges (yardage included above - 3 strips)
Leaf Applique	Purchase ½ yd of Tan (one fabric)
	Purchase ¾ yd of Steam A Seam II
Backing	Purchase ¾ yd, piece it to 26" x 46"
Batting	Purchase 26" x 46"
Embroidery	Purchase Tan Pearl Cotton floss for the leaf stems

Sewing machine, needle, thread

continued on pages 40 - 43

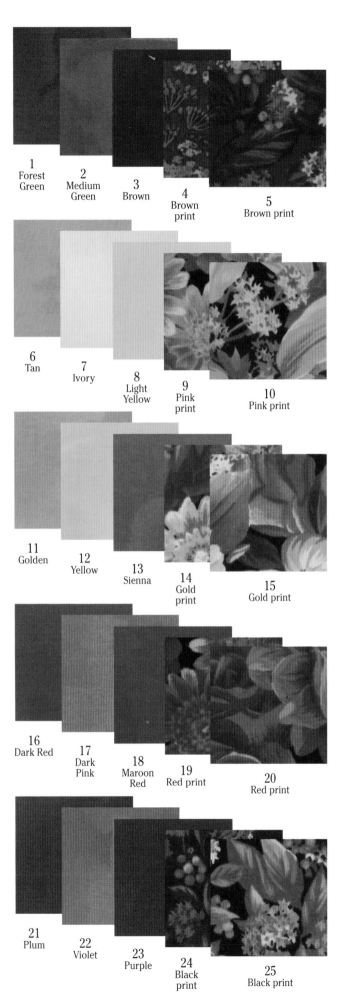

1 Forest Green
2 Medium Green
3 Brown
4 Brown print
5 Brown print

6 Tan
7 Ivory
8 Light Yellow
9 Pink print
10 Pink print

11 Golden
12 Yellow
13 Sienna
14 Gold print
15 Gold print

16 Dark Red
17 Dark Pink
18 Maroon Red
19 Red print
20 Red print

21 Plum
22 Violet
23 Purple
24 Black print
25 Black print

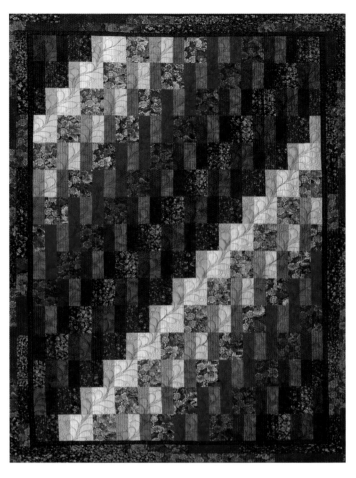

Flower Garden Quilt

Do you have a large collection of quarter yard pieces in your stash?

Whether you use what you have on hand or purchase fabrics, the striking contrasts, bold colors, and movement in the Flower Garden quilt make it a favorite.

The 'Bargello' technique makes it quick to piece. This quilt is definitely on the "most request-ed" list.

SIZE: 60" x 100"

Yardage

We purchased a *Moda* 'Ella' by Sentimental Studios. 'Fat Quarters' collection of fabrics.

Center ¼ yd each of 25 different fabrics
(3 strips 2½" x 42" of each - 75 strips total)

Outer Pieced Border
¼ yd each of 6 different dark fabrics
(3 strips 2½" x 42" of each - 18 strips total)

Inner Border and Binding
Purchase 1¼ yd Black marbled (15 strips - 42" long)

Backing 6 yds, piece it to 64" x 104"

Batting 64" x 104"

continued on pages 44 - 48

Butterflies and Birds

Butterflies and Birds provide an excellent opportunity to display your talent for machine appliqué.

SIZE: 44" x 64"

Yardage

TIP: We used leftover Piano Key Borders from the Flower Garden quilt (pages 14 - 15) to make the stripes in this quilt.

We purchased *Moda* 'Ella' by Sentimental Studios collection of fabrics.

Piano Key Stripes:
Purchase
1 strip 2½" x 21" of each fabric 1 - 25 from the Flower Garden Quilt on pages 14 - 15

Black Stripes
and Black Border:
Purchase
1½ yd of Black marbled

Border and Binding:
Purchase 1¼ yd of Floral print

Backing
Purchase 1½ yd, piece it to 48" x 68"

Batting
Purchase 48" x 68"

continued on pages 48 - 51

Folk Art Birds

Birds and flowers are traditional folk art appliqué motifs. These brilliant, eye-catching colors are sure to please your family and friends.

SIZE: 47" x 47"

Yardage

TIP: We used leftover Piano Key Borders from the Flower Garden quilt (pages 14 - 15) to make the stripes in this quilt.

We purchased *Moda* 'Ella' by Sentimental Studios collection of fabrics

Inner Border	¼ yd each of fabrics 8 thru 23 (1 strip of each 2½" x 15") See the color swatches on page 14.
Black Blocks and Corners	Purchase 1 yd of Black Marbled
Outer Border and Binding	Purchase 1½ yd of Floral print
Appliques	Purchase ¼ yd each of Dark Red, Golden, Yellow, Medium Green Purchase 1¼ yd of Steam A Seam II fusible web
Backing	Purchase 1⅔ yd, piece it to 51" x 51"
Batting	Purchase 51" x 51"

continued on pages 52 - 57

Birds & Blooms

Next time you need something cheerful, make this beautiful block. It's a great project that will be treasured for years to come.

SIZE: 32" x 32"

Yardage

TIP: We used leftover Piano Key Borders from the Flower Garden quilt (pages 14 - 15) to make the inner border.

We purchased *Moda 'Ella'* by Sentimental Studios collection of fabrics

Pieced Inner Border
        1 strip each 2½" x 21" of 7 Marbled fabrics
        Forest Green - Medium Green - Brown -
        Black print - Black print - Tan - Ivory

Center Square   Purchase ¼ yd Brown Marbled
Inner Border   Purchase ¼ yd Forest Green Marbled
Corner Squares, Outer Border and Binding
                        Purchase 1 yd Black prints
Applique:
    Purchase ¼ yd Medium Green Marbled for leaves and stems
    Purchase ¼ yd Dark Red Marbled for birds and flowers
    Purchase ¼ yd Golden Marbled for birds, beaks and flowers
    Purchase ⅛ yd Yellow Marbled for bird eyes
    Purchase 2 yd Steam A Seam fusible web

Backing   Purchase 1 yd, piece it to 36" x 36"

Batting   Purchase 36" x 36"

Sewing machine, needle, thread

continued on pages 19 - 21

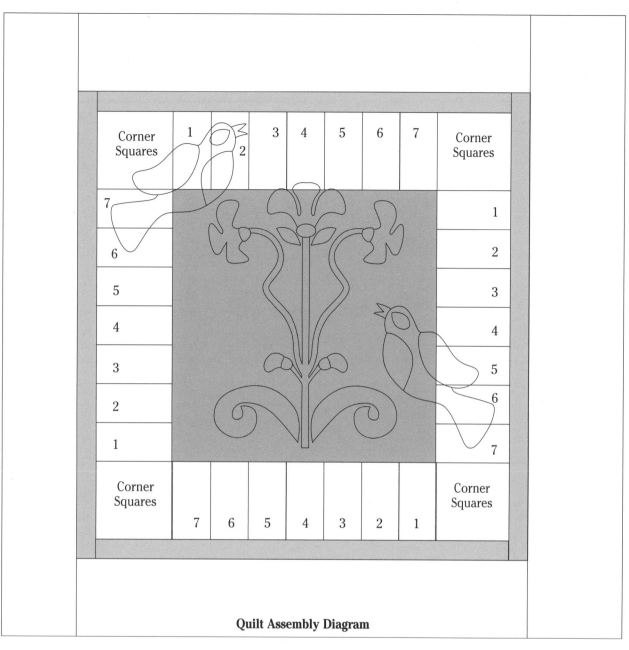

Quilt Assembly Diagram

Cutting

Piano Keys Inner Border:
Sew 2½" x 21" strips together in a color sequence from 1 through 7. Press.

    Forest Green - Medium Green - Brown -
    Black print - Black print - Cream - Ivory
Cut the 7-strip set into four pieces 4½" x 14½".
Center Block: Cut 1 Black square 14½" x 14½".
Corner Squares: Cut 4 Black print squares 4½" x 4½".

Assembly

See Quilt Diagram
Inner Pieced Border:
Position two 4½" wide 7-set strips, one on each side of the Center Block. Note the order of the colors. Sew a 7-set strip to each side. Press.

Sew a Corner Square to each end of two 4½" wide 7-set strips. Press.

Sew the two remaining strips (with Black print corners) to the top and bottom of the Center Block. Again note the sequence of the colors.

Borders

Green Border:
Cut 2 Forest Green strips 1½" x 22½" for the top and bottom. Sew to the top and bottom of the Center Block. Press.

Cut 2 side strips 1½" x 24½".
Sew to the sides of the Center Block. Press.

Outer Border:
Cut 2 Black print strips 4½" x 24½" for the top and bottom. Sew to the top and bottom of the quilt. Press.

Cut 2 side strips 4½" x 32½".
Sew to the sides of the quilt. Press.

Finishing

Applique: See Basic Instructions on page 58 - 61

Quilting: See Basic Instructions on page 60.

Binding: See Basic Instructions on page 60.
Cut 4 strips of Black print 2½" x 42". Sew end to end for 134" of binding.

continued from pages 18 - 19

Join to the
center flower
at the bottom
of this page

Join to
flower at
the top
of this
page

Center of flower pattern. Join to pattern on pages 22 - 23

continued from pages 20 - 21

Center of flower pattern. Join to pattern on pages 20 - 21

Reposition bird
above the flower
when you make
the quilt

Hearts A Flutter Quilt

see photos on pages 4 - 5

SIZE: 48" x 60"

Yardage

We used a *Moda* 'Chelsea' by Blackbird Designs.
'Jelly Roll' collection of pre-cut 2½" fabric strips
- we purchased 1 'Jelly Roll'.

Blocks: ½ yd of Reds OR 5 strips 2½" x 42"
1 yd of Greens OR 11 strips 2½" x 42"
¾ yd of Browns OR 8 strips 2½" x 42"
1½ yd of Tans OR 16 strips 2½" x 42"

Inner Border Browns (yardage included above - 5 strips)
Outer Borders Tans (yardage included above - 10 strips)
Binding Purchase ¼ yd Tans for 6 strips
Hearts Purchase ¼ yd Reds (3 strips 2½" x 42")
Backing Purchase 2¾ yds, piece it to 52" x 64"
Batting Purchase 52" x 64"
Freezer Paper for Applique, Sewing machine, needle, thread

Preparation

Block 1: Choose 11 Green strips and 1 Brown strip.

Block 2: Choose 6 Tan strips.

Block 3: Choose 5 Red strips and 1 Brown strip.

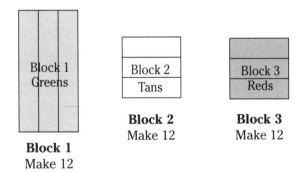

Block 1
Make 12

Block 2
Make 12

Block 3
Make 12

Blocks

1: Sew 4 sets of 3 Green/Brown strips together (2½" x 42"). Press.

2: Sew 2 sets of 3 Tan strips together (2½" x 42"). Press

3: Sew 2 sets of 3 Red/Brown strips together (2½" x 42"). Press.

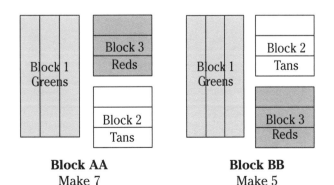

Block AA
Make 7

Block BB
Make 5

Block 1: Cut 4 Green/Brown 3-strip sets into 6½" x 12½" rectangles.

Block 2: Cut 2 Tan 3-strip sets into 6½" squares.

Block 3: Cut 2 Red/Brown 3-strip sets into 6½" squares.

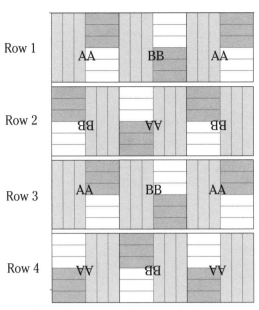

Row 1 — AA BB AA

Row 2 — BB AA BB

Row 3 — AA BB AA

Row 4 — AA BB AA

Turn Rows 2 and 4 upside down.

Assembly

See Block Diagram.
Make 7 of Block AA.
Make 5 of Block BB.

See Quilt Diagram.
Sew 3 sets of Blocks AA - BB - AA together to form rows 1 - 3 and 4.
Sew 1 set of Blocks BB - AA - BB together to form row 2.
Press.

Arrange rows.
Turn Rows 2 and 4 upside down .
Sew the rows together. Press.

Borders

Brown - Inner Border:
Randomly sew 5 Brown strips end to end for 180".
Cut 2 side strips 2½" x 48½".
Cut 2 strips 2½" x 40½" for top and bottom.
Sew the side strips to the quilt. Press.
Sew the top and bottom borders to the quilt. Press.

Tan Outer Borders:
Sew 10 Tan strips end to end for 408".

Tan - First Outer Border:
Cut 2 side strips 2½" x 52½"
Cut 2 strips 2½" x 44½" for top and bottom.

Sew the side strips to the quilt. Press.
Sew the top and bottom borders to the quilt. Press.

Tan - Second Outer Border:
Cut 2 side strips 2½" x 56½".
Cut 2 strips 2½" x 48½" for top and bottom.

Sew the side strips to the quilt. Press.
Sew the top and bottom strips to the quilt. Press.

Applique Hearts

Cut Red strips into 6 strips 2½" x 21". Sew Red strips together side by side to make three 2-strip sets. Press.

Hearts:

See Basic Instructions for Freezer Paper Applique on page 58.

Cut out 12 hearts from freezer paper.

Align freezer paper hearts at an angle on the 2-strip sets and press to the back of fabric.

Cut out fabric hearts adding a ⅛" border all around the freezer paper.

Remove the freezer paper and turn it over so the waxy side is up.

Center paper on the back of the fabric heart and press the ⅛" border to the waxy paper to make a hem.

Press firmly.

Carefully remove the paper, preserving the hem.

Position the hearts. Blindstitch each one in place on a Tan block.

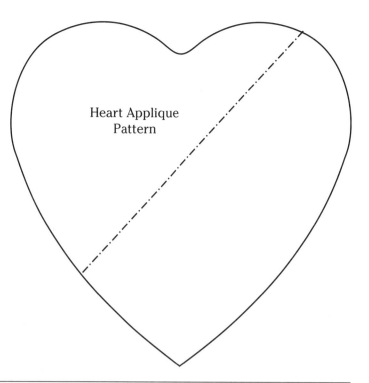

Heart Applique Pattern

Finishing

Quilting:

See Basic Instructions on pages 58 - 61.

Binding:

See Basic Instructions on page 61.

Sew 6 Tan strips end to end to make 220" of binding.

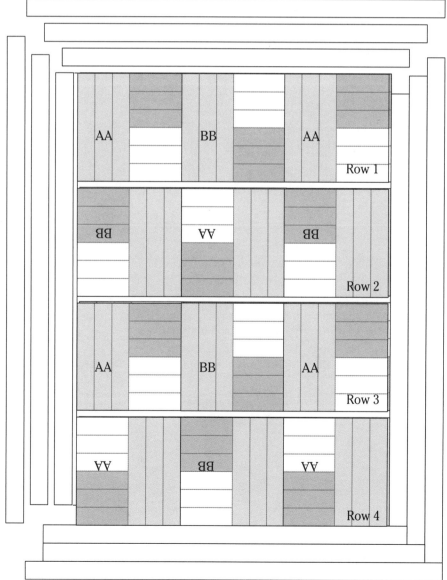

Turn Rows 2 and 4 upside down

Bluebirds of Happiness Quilt

photos on pages 6 - 7

SIZE: 34" x 48"

Yardage

We purchased *Moda* 'Folklorique' by Fig Tree
Purchase the following fabrics:
Center of Quilt
¾ yd of Greens (8 strips 2½" x 42")
¾ yd of Oranges (8 strips 2½" x 42")
Inner Border and Bluebirds
½ yd of Blues (3 strips 2½" x 42")
Piano Keys Outer Border
¾ yd of Creams/Beiges (10 strips 2½" x 42")
Binding
Oranges (yardage included above - 5 strips)
Applique
Blues (yardage included above)
¼ yd of Brown (2 strips 2½" x 42")
Purchase 1 yd of Steam A Seam II

Backing   Purchase 1½ yd, piece it to 38" x 52"
Batting   Purchase 38" x 52"
Sewing machine, needle, thread

Assemble the Center

Center Strips:
Cut 8 Green strips 2½" x 36½"
Cut 3 Orange strips 2½" x 36½"

Sew center strips together:
1 Orange - 4 Green - 1 Orange - 4 Green - 1 Orange.
Press.

Borders

Blue Inner Border:
Cut 2 strips 1½" x 36½" for the sides.
Cut 2 strips 1½" x 24½" for the top and bottom

Sew 1½" x 36½"strips to the sides of quilt. Press.
Sew 1½" x 24½"strips to the top and bottom.
Press.

Sew 19 strips to make a strip 10½" x 38½"

Cut 10½" x 38½" strip into two strips, each 5" x 38½"

Cream/Beige Piano Keys Border:
Cut 19 strips 2½" x 10½".
Cut Strips for the Sides:
Sew the 19 strips side by side to make a strip 10½" x 38½".
Press.
Cut the 10½" x 38½" strip into two strips, each 5" x 38½".

Sew 17 strips to make a strip 10½" x 34½"

Cut one 10½" x 34½" strip into two strips, each 5" x 34½"

Cut Strips for the Top and Bottom:
Cut 17 strips 2½" x 10½"
Sew 17 strips 2½" x 10½" to make a strip 10½" x 34½". Press.
Cut the 10½" x 34½" strip into two strips, each 5" x 34½".

Sew Strips to Quilt:
Sew a 5" x 38½" strip to each side of the quilt. Press
Sew a 5" x 34½" strip to the top and bottom of the quilt.
Press.
Trim off excess fabric.

Finishing

Applique: See Basic Instructions on page 58 - 61
Quilting: See Basic Instructions on page 60.
Binding: See Basic Instructions on page 60.
Cut 5 Orange strips 2½" x 40" and sew end to end for
168" of binding.

17 strips in the top and bottom borders

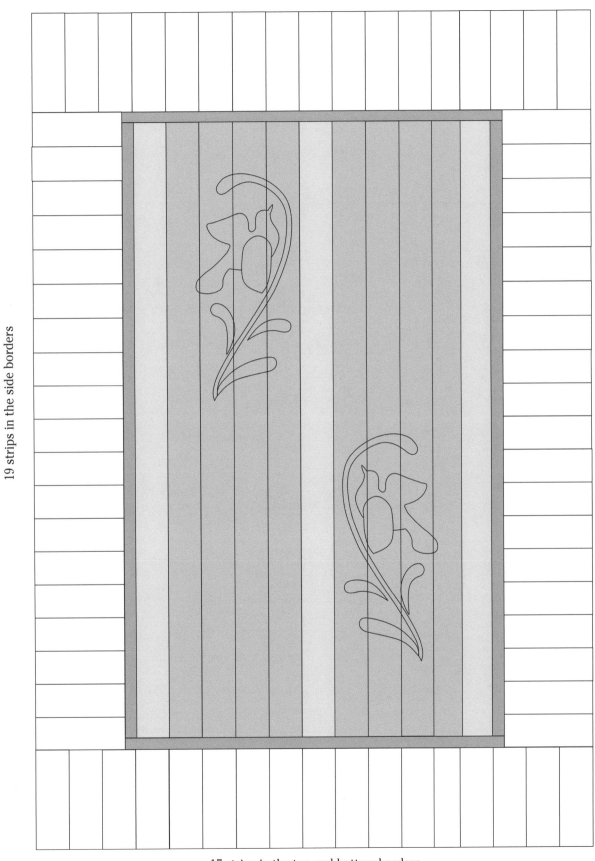

19 strips in the side borders

19 strips in the side borders

17 strips in the top and bottom borders

Bluebirds Quilt Assembly Diagram

continued on pages 28 - 31

continued from pages 26 - 27

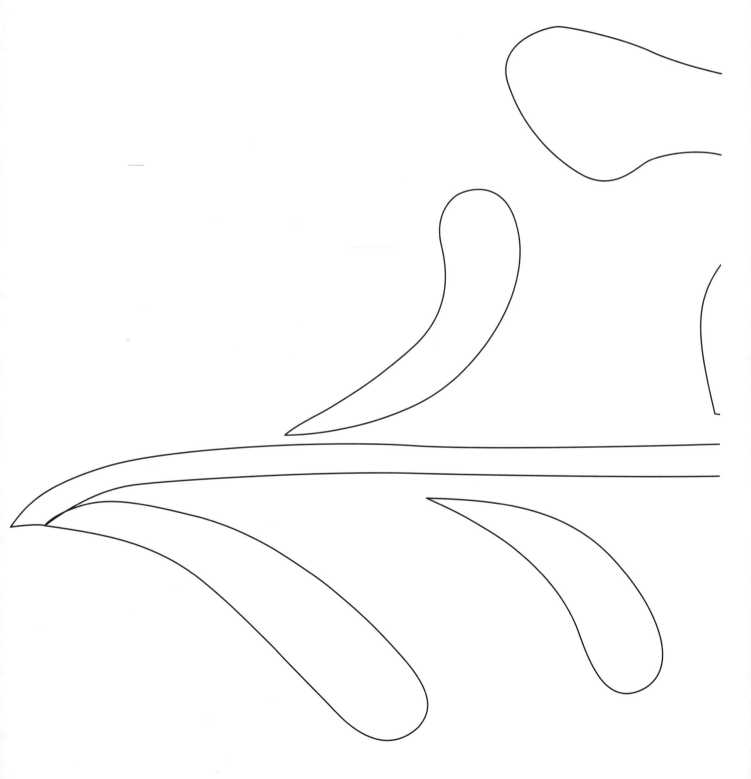

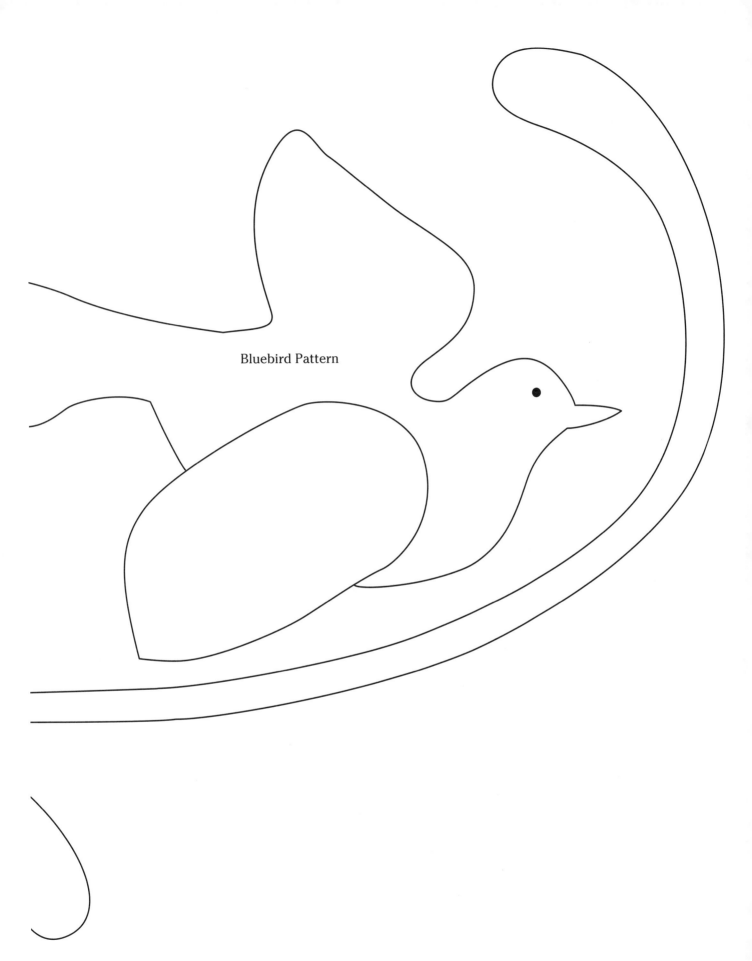

Bluebird Pattern

continued on pages 30 - 31

continued from pages 26 - 27

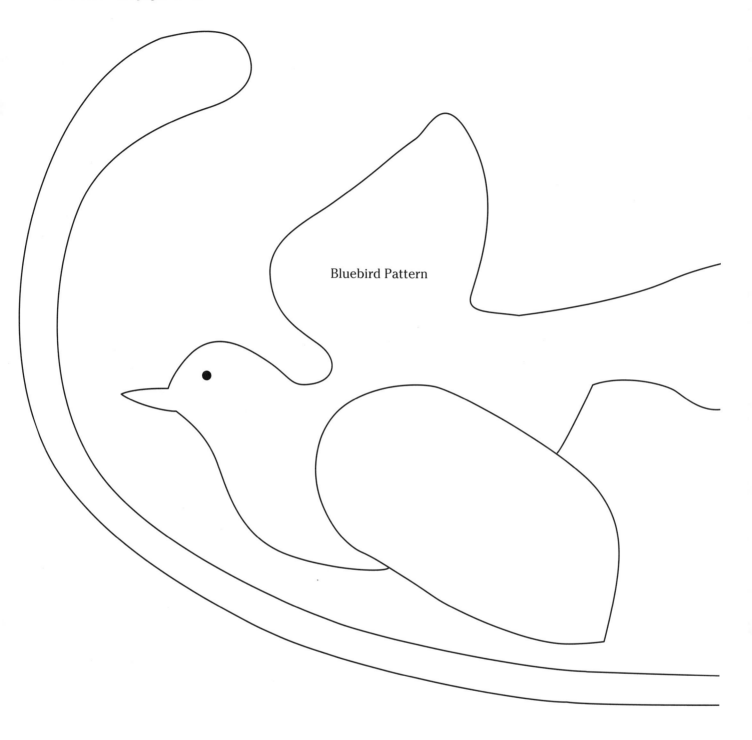

Bluebird Pattern

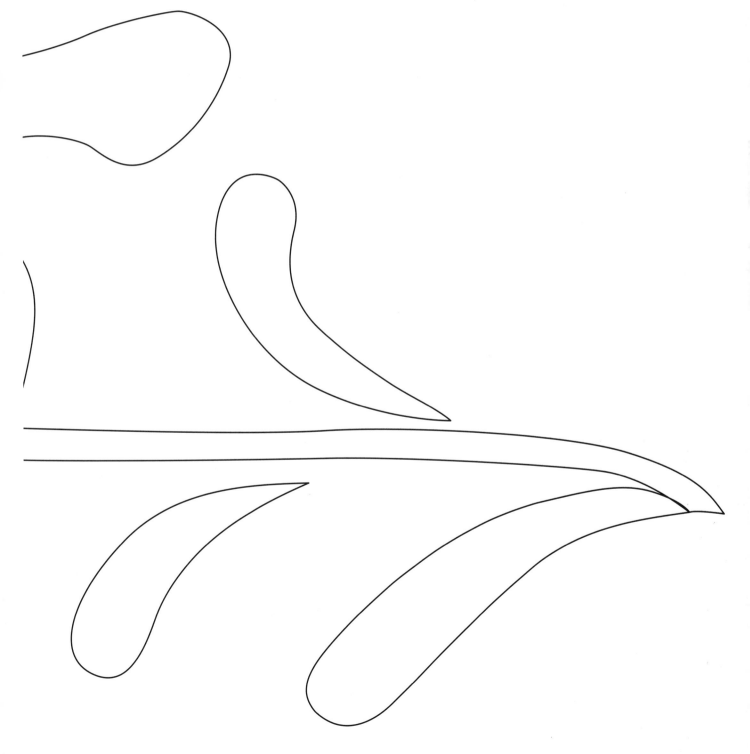

Spring Showers Quilt

photos are on pages 8 - 9

SIZE: 44" x 60"

Yardage

We used *Moda* 'Sanctuary' by 3 Sisters
'Jelly Roll' collection of pre-cut 2½" fabric strips
- we purchased 1 'Jelly Roll'.

Flower Blocks
- ½ yd of Purples OR 5 strips 2½" x 42"
- 1 yd of Ivory OR 11 strips 2½" x 42"
- ½ yd of Yellows OR 6 strips 2½" x 42"
- ½ yd of Greens OR 6 strips 2½" x 42"
- ½ yd of Pinks OR 5 strips 2½" x 42"

Leaf Applique
- Greens (yardage included above - 3 strips)

Gathered Flower Applique
- ¼ yd of Reds (or 2 strips 2½" x 42")
- Yellows (yardage included above - 2 strips)
- Purples (yardage included above - 2 strips)

Border and Binding
- Purchase 1¹2 yd of Green print

Backing Purchase 1¼ yds, piece it to 48" x 64"
Batting Purchase 48" x 64"

Dritz Buttons to Cover
- Six 1⅝" diameter
- Twelve 1¼" diameter
  - Note: Do not use buttons on a quilt that will be used by babies or toddlers. Substitute Yo-Yo circles.

Sewing machine, needle, thread

Cutting

Borders for each Block:

Cut Greens for Blocks 1 and 4.
Cut Pinks for Blocks 3 and 6.
Cut Yellows for Block 2.
Cut Purples for Block 5.
- 1 of strip D: 2½" x 12½" (6 total) for top and bottom
- 2 of strip E: 2½" x 14½" (12 total) for sides
- 1 of strip F: 2½" x 16½" (6 total) for sides

Flower Pots for each Block:

Purple: 6 of strip A for Blocks 1, 4, & 5: 2½" x 4½"
Pink: 6 of strip A for Blocks 2, 3, & 6: 2½" x 4½"

Light Backgrounds for each Block:

Cut from Ivory with lighter prints:
- 4 of strip B: 2½" x 4½" (24 total)

Cut from Ivory with darker prints:
- 4 of strip C: 2½" x 12½" (24 total)

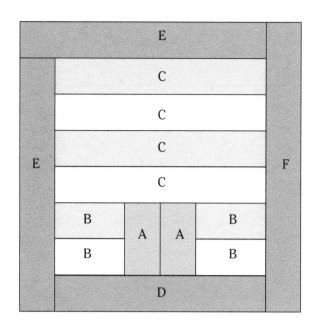

Sew Centers of Blocks

Sew 1 set of strip A's together. Press.
Sew 2 sets of strip B's together. Press.
Sew sets BB - AA - BB, noting direction of the seams. Press.
Sew 4 strip C's together, alternating the colors. Press.
Sew the CCCC set to the BB - AA - BB set. Press.

Sew Borders to Blocks

Block Border Colors:
- Block 1: Green
- Block 2: Yellow
- Block 3: Pink
- Block 4: Green
- Block 5: Purple
- Block 6: Pink

Sew strip D to the top and bottom of each block. Press.
  TIP: Refer to color listing above.
Sew strips E to the side and top of each block. Press.
Sew strip F to the remaining side of each block. Press.

Assemble Blocks

See Quilt Diagram.
Sew blocks to make 3 rows of 2 blocks each. Press.
Sew the rows together. Press.

Quilt Border

Cut 2 Green print borders 6½" x 48½" for the sides.
Sew to the sides of the quilt. Press.
Cut 2 Green print borders 6½" x 44½" for the top and bottom.
Sew to the top and bottom of the quilt. Press.

Finishing

Quilting: See Basic Instructions on pages 58 - 61.

Binding: See Basic Instructions on page 60.
Cut 6 strips 2½" x 40" and sew end to end for 214" of binding.

Applique: See pages 34 - 35 for leaves, flowers and centers.

Spring Showers Quilt Diagram and Flowers Placement

continued on pages 34 - 35

continued from pages 32 - 33

Pillow

continued from pages 8 - 9

SIZE: 16" x 16"

We used leftover strips from *Moda* 'Sanctuary'.

Pillow Top
¼ yd Ivory OR 2 strips 2½" x 42"
¼ yd Reds OR 2 strips 2½" x 42"

Applique
1 of each strip 2½" x 21" (Red, Yellow, Purple)
1 Green strip 2½" x 21"

Backing   Purchase ¾ yd
Purchase Polyfil or Layers of Batting for stuffing

3 *Dritz* 1¼" diameter Buttons to Cover
Extra fabric for Buttons or Yo-Yos

Cutting

Cut Red strips:
2 strip A: 2½" x 4½"
1 strip D: 2½" x 12½"
2 strip E: 2½" x 14½"
1 strip F: 2½" x 16½"

Cut White strips:
4 strip B: 2½" x 4½"
4 strip C: 2½" x 12½"

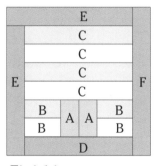

Assembly

Sew strips together as shown.

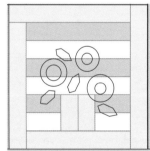

Finishing

Applique:
Add Leaves, Gathered Flowers, Buttons or Yo-Yos.

Backing:
Cut 2 rectangles 16½" x 24".

Fold back a 3" hem along one 16" side of each rectangle. Topstitch the hem.

Overlap the hems in the middle, making a 16½" x 16½" square. With right sides together, align the raw edges of the 2 backings with the edges of the pillow.

Sew all around the pillow.

Turn the pillow right side out so you can stuff it through the overlap opening.

Add stuffing or folded quilt batting in the shape of the pillow.

24"

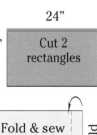

16"

Cut 2 rectangles

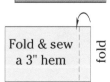

Fold & sew a 3" hem

fold

Overlap backings

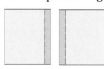

Applique
for Quilt and Pillow

Make Leaves, Flowers and Centers:

Make 4 Leaves for each block, a total of 24 Leaves.

Make 3 Gathered Flowers for each block, a total of 18 flowers.

Make a Covered Button or Yo-Yo for the center of each Flower, a total of 18 centers.

Add to Blocks:

Sew 3 Flowers to each block.

Sew 4 Leaves to each block.

Sew a center to each Flower.

Leaves and Flowers

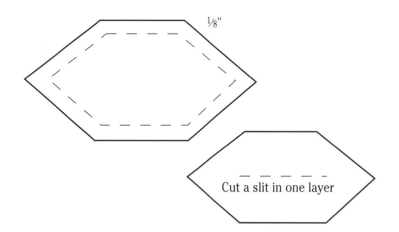

Applique Leaves:

Fold Green fabric with right sides together. Mark each leaf pattern.

Cut out 4 leaves for each block using the pattern (24 for quilt, 5 for pillow).

Sew around each leaf ⅛" from the edge.

Carefully slit one Green layer. Turn each leaf right side out through the slit.

Position leaves on each block. Pin and Blindstitch in place.

⅛"

Cut a slit in one layer

Gathered Flowers:

Cut 6 strips of Red 2½" x 8".

Cut 6 strips of Yellow 2½" x 8".

Cut 6 strips of Purple 2½" x 8".

Fold each strip in half lengthwise with wrong sides together.

Sew a Gathering stitch ⅛" from the raw edge. Gather tightly.

Join the ends into a circle.

Position each flower on quilt top. Pin and Blindstitch in place.

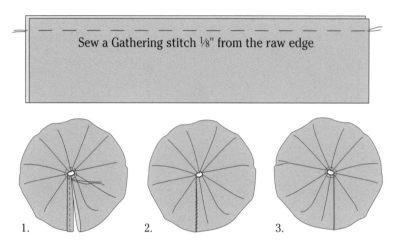

Sew a Gathering stitch ⅛" from the raw edge

1. 2. 3.

Gathered Flowers Diagrams

Yo-Yo Centers:

Make a Yo-Yo for the center of each flower.

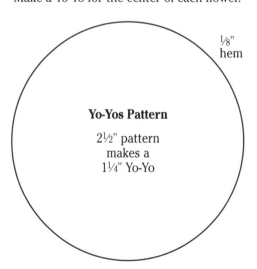

⅛"
hem

Yo-Yos Pattern

2½" pattern
makes a
1¼" Yo-Yo

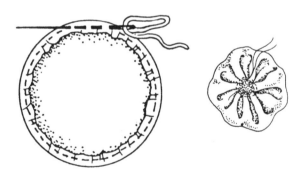

Yo-Yos: Make a cardboard circle template for Yo-Yos. Draw around the template onto the back of fabric. Cut out. Thread a needle with heavy duty thread. Turn the raw edges under ⅛" and gather with a Running stitch. Pull tight. Tie off and clip the thread.

Attach Yo-Yos: Pin a Yo-Yo in the center of each flower. Blindstitch the edges, make a Running stitch or tack in several places.

Covered Button Centers:

You'll need 6 squares 3" x 3" to cover the large buttons, and 12 squares 2½" x 2½" for small buttons. Cover buttons by following directions on the package.

Sew one in the center of each flower.

Note: Do not use real buttons on a quilt that will be used by babies or toddlers. Substitute Yo-Yo circles.

Cranes Quilt

continued from pages 10 - 11

SIZE: 54" x 74"

Yardage

We purchased *Moda* 'Koi Garden' by Sentimental Studios collection of fabrics.

Blocks
> Purchase 2¼ yd of Oranges (26 strips 2½" x 42")

First Block Border
> Purchase 1¾ yd Navy Blues (22 strips 2½" x 42")

Second Block Border - Sashing
> Purchase ¾ yd Tans and prints (8 strips 2½" x 42")

Inner Quilt Border and Corners
> Purchase ¾ yd Black marbled (7 strips)

Second Quilt Border
> Oranges (yardage included above - 6 strips)

Outside Quilt Border
> Oranges (yardage included above - 4 strips)
> Navy Blues (yardage included above - 4 strips)

Binding
> Navy Blues (yardage included above - 7 strips)

Applique Cranes
> Black Swirl or Black Marbled (yardage included above)
> ¼ yd of Tan Feather
> ¼ yd of White
> ¼ yd of Red
> Purchase 1¼ yd of Steam A Seam II fusible web

Backing   Purchase 3 yds pieced to 58" x 78"
Batting   Purchase 58" x 78"

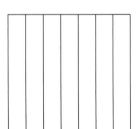

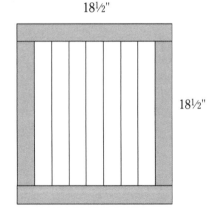

18½"

18½"

Blocks

Blocks:
> Cut 42 Orange print strips 2½" x 14½".
> Sew a set of 7 Orange strips side by side for each Block. Press.

First Block Border - Navy Blue
> Cut 12 Navy Blue strips 2½" x 14½" for the sides.
> Cut 12 Navy Blue strips 2½" x 18½" for the top and bottom.
>
> Sew a Navy Blue 2½" x 14½" strip to each side. Press.
> Sew a Navy Blue 2½" x 18½" strip to each side. Press.

Second Block Border - Tan Sashing:
> Corners: Cut 12 Black 2½" x 2½" squares.
> Strips: Cut 17 Tan strips 2½" x 18½".

Assemble the Blocks

See Quilt Diagram.

Sew 3 rows of Blocks together:
> Tan strip - Block - Tan strip - Block - Tan strip (18½" x 42½"). Press.

Sew 4 Horizontal Sashing:
> Black 2½" square - Tan 2½" x 18½" strip - Black square - Tan strip - Black square (2½" x 42½"). Press.

Sew Blocks and Sashing together:
> Sew a horizontal sash between each row as shown in the Quilt Diagram. Press.

Quilt Borders

Black Inner Border:
Cut 6 Black strips 2½" x 42".
Sew Black strips end to end to make 252".

Cut 2 strips 2½" x 62½" for the sides.
Cut 2 strips 2½" x 46½" for the top and bottom.

Sew the side borders to the quilt. Press.
Sew the top and bottom borders. Press.

Second Pieced Border:
Cut 6 Orange strips 2½" x 42".
Sew Orange strips end to end to make 252" of border.

Cut 2 strips 2½" x 66½" for the sides.
Cut 2 strips 2½" x 50½" for the top and bottom.

Sew the side borders to the quilt. Press.
Add the top and bottom borders. Press.

Outer Checkerboard Border:
Cut 4 Navy Blue strips 2½" x 42".
Cut 4 Orange strips 2½" x 42".
Sew 4 Navy strips and 4 Orange strips together side by side, repeating Navy - Orange - Navy - Orange - etc.
Now cut the length into 2½" x 16½" checkerboard strips.
> Sew together end to end.

Cut 2 strips 2½" x 70½" for the sides.
Cut 2 strips 2½" x 54½" for the top and bottom.

Sew the side borders to the quilt. Press.
Add the top and bottom borders. Press.

Finishing

Applique:
See Basic Instructions on page 58 - 61
Quilting:
See Basic Instructions on page 60.
Binding:
See Basic Instructions on page 61.
Cut 7 strips 2½" x 42". Sew strips end to end
for 260" of binding.

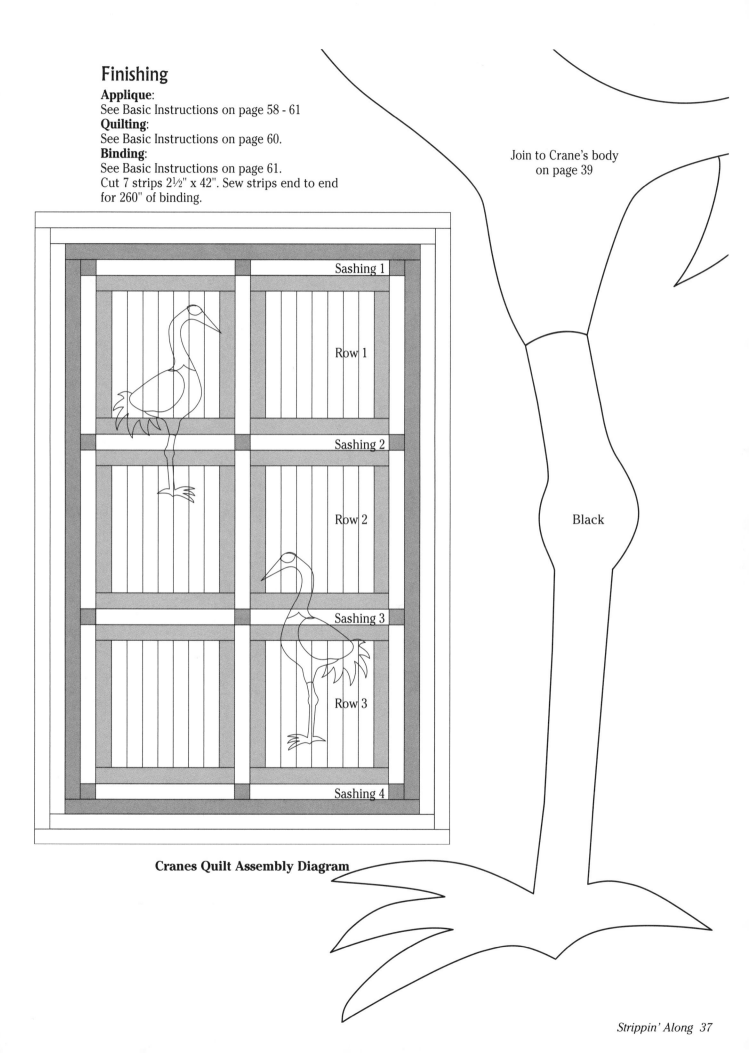

Join to Crane's body
on page 39

Black

Sashing 1

Row 1

Sashing 2

Row 2

Sashing 3

Row 3

Sashing 4

Cranes Quilt Assembly Diagram

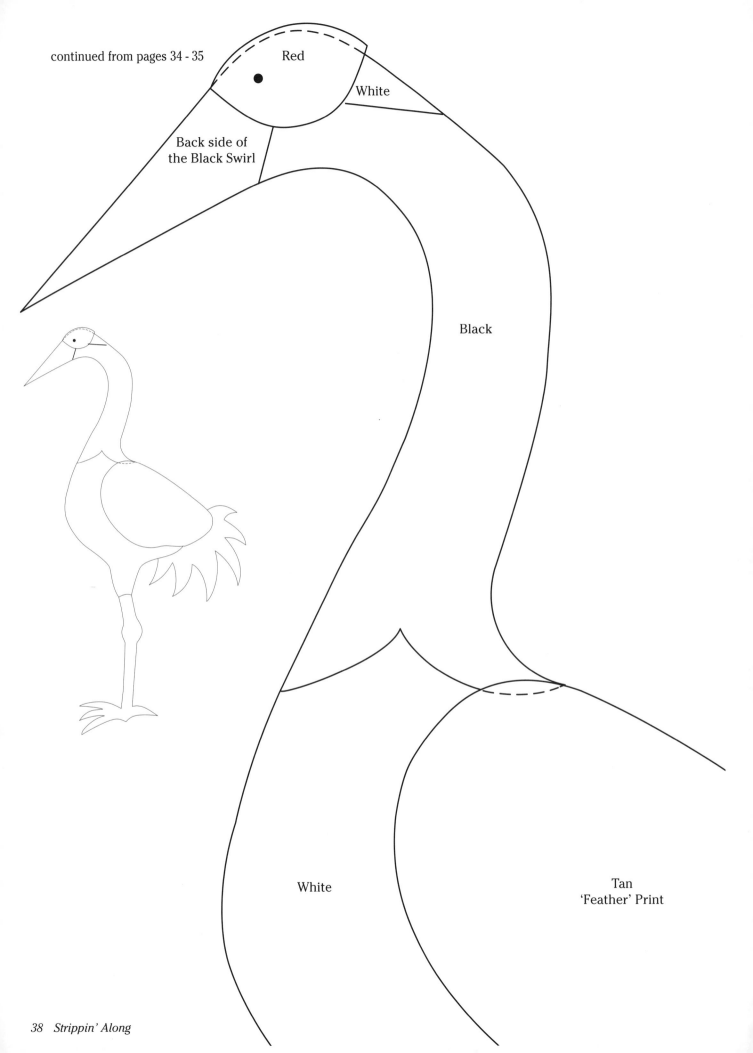

continued from pages 34 - 35

Red

White

Back side of
the Black Swirl

Black

White

Tan
'Feather' Print

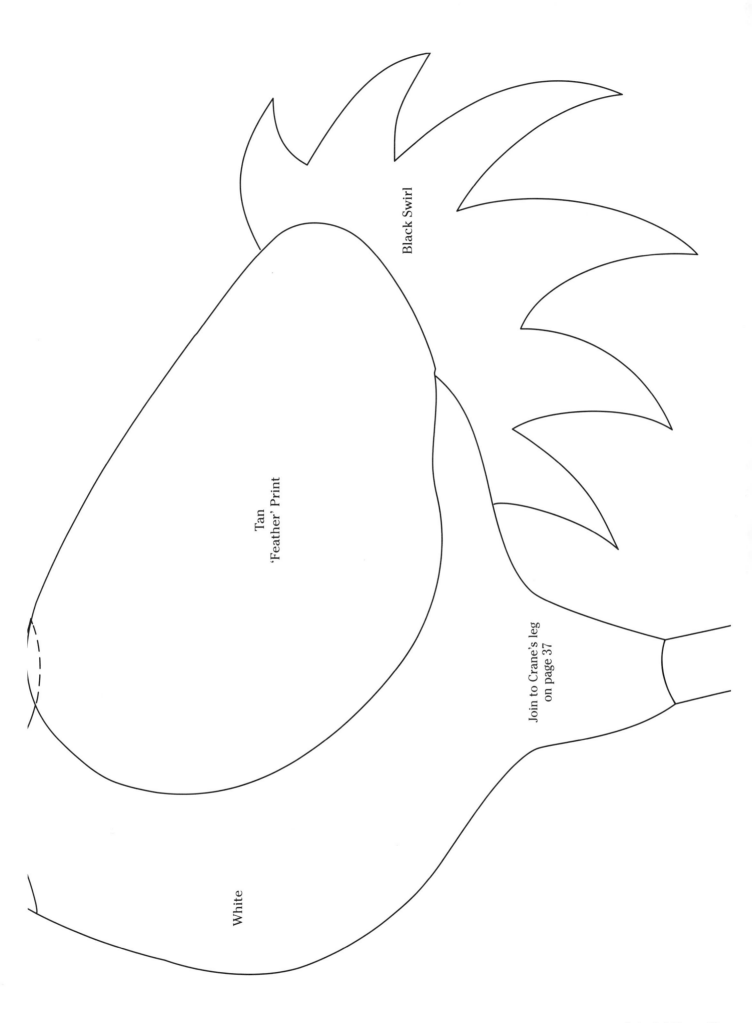

Black Swirl

Tan
'Feather' Print

White

Join to Crane's leg
on page 37

Note: We use the same Basic Instructions for assembling the Blocks.

Koi for Good Luck Quilt

continued from page 12

SIZE: 54" x 54"

Yardage

We purchased *Moda* Koi Garden by Sentimental Studios.
collection of fabrics, see page 10

Blocks	2½ yd of Red/Oranges (25 strips 2½" x 42")
Block Borders	1¼ yd of Browns (15 strips 2½" x 42")
Sashing	½ yd of Tans (4 strips 2½" x 42")
Sashing Corners	⅛ yd of Black (1 strip 2½" x 42")
Piano Keys Border	Red/Oranges (yardage included above - 8 strips)
	Browns (yardage included above - 8 strips)
Binding:	Red/Oranges ((yardage included above - 6 strips)
Backing	Purchase 2½ yds, piece it to 58" x 58"
Batting	Purchase 58" x 58"

Sewing machine, needle, thread

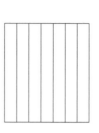
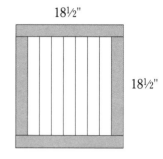

18½"

18½"

18½"

Leaves Table Topper

continued from page 13

SIZE: 22" x 42"

Yardage

We purchased *Moda* Koi Garden by Sentimental Studios.
collection of fabrics, see page 10

Blocks	¾ yd of 6 Red/Oranges (9 strips 2½" x 42")
Block Borders	½ yd of Browns (4 strips 2½" x 42")
Corners	⅛ yd of Black (1 strip 2½" x 42")
Sashing Strips	½ yd of Tans (4 strips 2½" x 42")
Binding:	Red/Oranges (yardage included above - 3 strips)
Leaf Applique	Purchase ½ yd of Tan (one fabric)
	Purchase ¾ yd of Steam A Seam II
Backing	Purchase ¾ yd, piece it to 26" x 46"
Batting	Purchase 26" x 46"
Embroidery	Purchase Tan Pearl Cotton floss for the leaf stems

Sewing machine, needle, thread

Koi Quilt and Leaves Topper:

Basic Instructions for assembling the Blocks

Blocks

Blocks:
Cut Red/Orange strips 2½" x 14½"
(28 for Koi quilt, 14 for Leaves topper).
Sew a set of 7 Orange strips side by side for
each Block. Press.

First Block Border - Brown
Cut Brown strips 2½" x 14½" for the sides.
(8 for Koi quilt, 4 for Leaves topper)
Cut Brown strips 2½" x 18½" for the top
and bottom.
(8 for Koi quilt, 4 for Leaves topper)
Sew a Brows 2½" x 14½" strip to each side.
Press.
Sew a Brown 2½" x 18½" strip to each side.
Press.

Second Block Border - Tan Sashing:
Corners: Cut Black 2½" x 2½" squares.
(9 for Koi quilt, 6 for Leaves topper)
Strips: Cut Tan strips 2½" x 18½".
(12 for Koi quilt, 7 for Leaves topper)

Assemble the Blocks

See Quilt or Topper Diagram.

Sew Rows of Blocks together:
Tan strip - Block - Tan strip - Block - Tan strip
(18½" x 42½"). Press.
(2 rows for Koi quilt, 1 row for Leaves topper)

Sew Horizontal Sashing:
Black 2½" square - Tan 2½" x 18½" strip -
Black square - Tan strip - Black square (2½" x
42½"). Press.
(3 rows for Koi quilt, 2 rows for Leaves topper)

Sew Blocks and Sashing together:
Sew a horizontal sash between each row as
shown in the Diagram. Press.

Sew 21 strips to make a strip 14" x 42½"

Cut 14" x 42½" strip into two strips, each 6½" x 42½"

You will also have a length of 27 strips to make a strip 14" x 54½"

You will cut the length of 27 strips to make 2 strips 6½" x 54½"

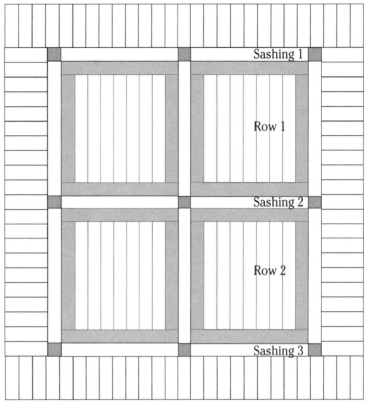

Sashing 1

Row 1

Sashing 2

Row 2

Sashing 3

'Koi for good Luck' Quilt Diagram

Koi Quilt: Piano Keys Border

Prepare Strips for Piano Keys Border:
Cut 9 Red/Orange strips 2½" x 42".
Cut 9 Brown strips 2½" x 42".
Sew Red/Orange strips end to end.
Sew Brown strips end to end.

Sew Piano Keys Border for Sides:
Cut 10 Red/Orange strips 2½" x 14".
Cut 11 Brown strips 2½" x 14".
Sew strips side to side alternating Red/Orange and Brown. You will have a 21-strip set 14" x 42½".
Cut 21-strip set into 2 pieces, each 6½" x 42½".

Sew Piano Keys Border for Sides:
Cut 13 Red/Orange strips 2½" x 14".
Cut 14 Brown strips 2½" x 14".
Sew strips side to side alternating Red/Orange and Brown. You will have a 27-strip set 14" x 54½".
Cut 27-strip set into 2 pieces, each 6½" x 54½".

Piano Keys Outer Borders:
Sew 21-strip set borders to the sides. Press.
Sew 27-strip set borders to the top and bottom. Press.

Finishing

Quilting:
See Basic Instructions on pages 58 - 61.
Binding:
See Basic Instructions on page 60.
Cut 6 Red/Orange strips 2½" x 42". Sew strips end to end for 220" of binding.

Leaves Topper: Finishing

Quilting:
See Basic Instructions on pages 58 - 61.
Binding:
See Basic Instructions on page 60.
Cut 3 Red/Orange strips 2½" x 42" plus 10" of scraps. Sew strips end to end for 134" of binding.

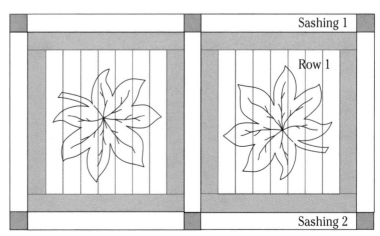

Sashing 1

Row 1

Sashing 2

Table Topper Diagram

continued from page 41

Leaf Pattern
for Table Topper

Cut 2

Leaf Pattern
for Table Topper

Cut 2

Flower Garden Quilt

photos are on pages 14 - 15

SIZE: 60" x 100"

Yardage

We purchased a *Moda* 'Ella' by Sentimental Studios. 'Fat Quarters' collection of fabrics.

Center   ¼ yd each of 25 different fabrics
             (3 strips 2½" x 42" of each - 75 strips total)

Outer Pieced Border
             ¼ yd each of 6 different dark fabrics
             (3 strips 2½" x 42" of each - 18 strips total)

Inner Border and Binding
             Purchase 1¼ yd Black marbled (15 strips - 42" long)

Backing   6 yds, piece it to 64" x 104"

Batting   64" x 104"

Construction Method
Tips:

There are 2 ways to construct this quilt. Choose the one that is easiest for you.

Take care to insure that, after sewing, each block is exactly 2" wide or your sections will not match. Measure and adjust as you go.

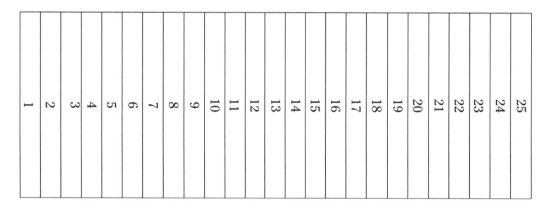

Construction Method 1:
Preparation for Strip Sets

Arrange 25 prints in a pleasing pattern. (We arranged ours in numerical order, 1 - 2 - 3 - 4 - 5 - 6 - 7 - 8 - 9 - 10 - 11 - 12 - 13 - 14 - 15 - 16 - 17 - 18 - 19 - 20 - 21 - 22 - 23 - 24 - 25.)

See the color samples on page 14.

Number each color of strip to avoid confusion.

Cut 5 strips of each fabric 2½" x 21".

Sew Strip Sets

Sew the 2½" x 21" strips side by side in sequence 1 thru 25.

You will have five 25-strip sets that are 50½" long. Press.

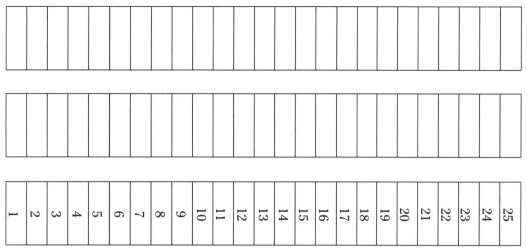

Row 1 - At the Top

Cut each 25-strip set (21" x 50½") into 3 sections, each 6½" x 50½".
Each 6½" x 50½" section will become a horizontal row.

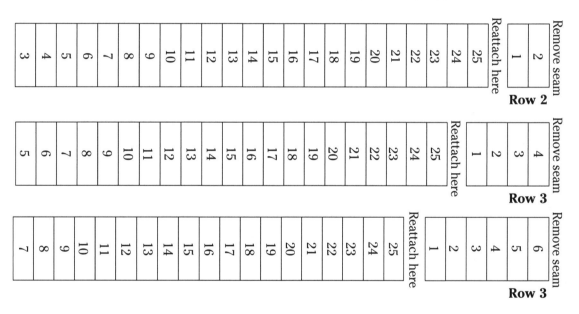

Row 2

Row 3

Row 3

For each row except Row 1, take out 1 seam after the first 2 rows.

Shift the piece to the end of the row and sew it in its new position.

This method requires a little extra work taking out and resewing the seams, but I think it is less confusing than Method 2.

Continue in this same manner with all five 25-strip sets (each 20" x 50½") until you have a total of 15 rows.

Be sure to shift every row by 2 colors to create the beautiful Bargello effect.

Construction Method 2

Cut each fabric into 15 strips 2½" x 6½".

Sew each piece into its individual location in each of the 15-strip sets.

In this method, you will sew 375 small individual pieces. I find this harder to keep up with than Method 1.

continued on pages 46 - 47

continued from pages 44 - 45

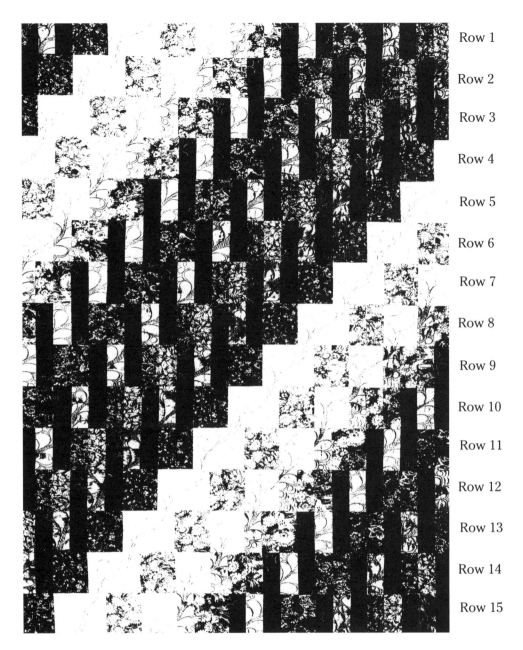

Row 1
Row 2
Row 3
Row 4
Row 5
Row 6
Row 7
Row 8
Row 9
Row 10
Row 11
Row 12
Row 13
Row 14
Row 15

Assembly

Refer to the Quilt Diagram.
Lay out each row of the 25-strip sets in sequence.
You will have a total of 15 rows. Press. Sew the rows together. Press.

Borders

Black Inner Border:
Cut 8 Black strips 1½" x 42". Sew end to end for 336".

Cut 2 strips 1½" x 90½" for the sides.
Cut 2 strips 1½" x 52½" for the top and bottom.

Sew 1½" x 90½"strips to the sides of the quilt. Press.
Sew 1½" x 52½" strips to the top and bottom. Press.

Pieced Borders:
Cut into 16 strips 2½" x 42" for the pieced borders.
Sew end to end.

Inner Pieced Border:
Cut 2 strips 2½" x 92½" for the sides.
Cut 2 strips 2½" x 56½" for the top and bottom.

Sew strips to the sides of the quilt.
Sew strips to the top and bottom.

Outer Pieced Border:
Cut 2 strips 2½" x 96½" for the sides.
Cut 2 strips 2½" x 60½" for the top and bottom.

Sew strips to the sides of the quilt. Press.
Sew strips to the top and bottom. Press.

Finishing

Quilting: See Basic Instructions on pages 58 - 61.
Binding: See Basic Instructions on page 60.
Cut 9 Black strips 2½" x 42" and sew them end to end to make 324" of binding.

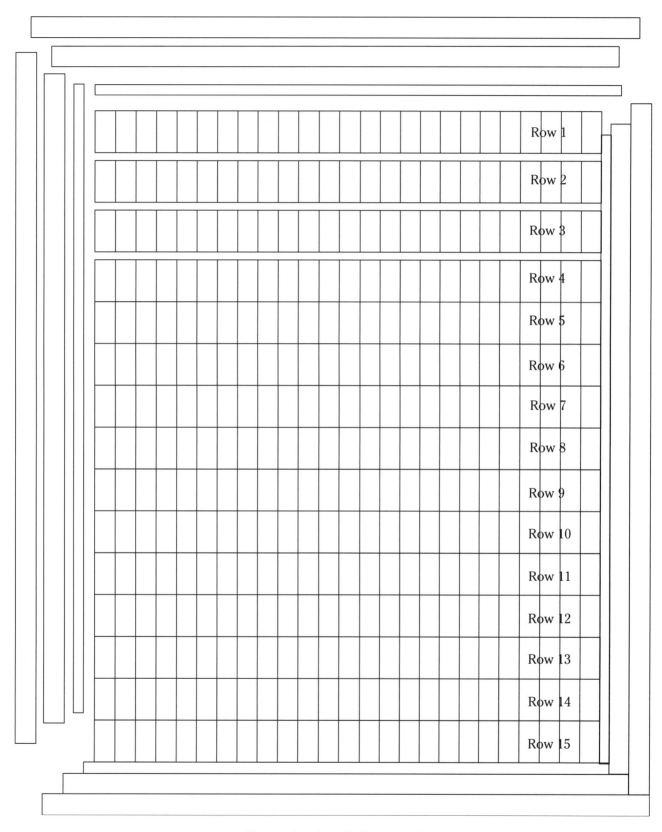

Row 1

Row 2

Row 3

Row 4

Row 5

Row 6

Row 7

Row 8

Row 9

Row 10

Row 11

Row 12

Row 13

Row 14

Row 15

Flower Garden Quilt Assembly

Butterflies & Birds Quilt

continued from page 16

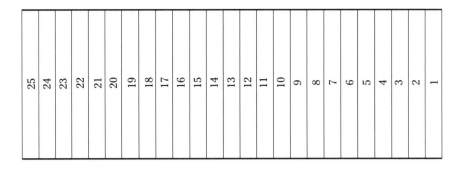

SIZE: 44" x 64"

Yardage

TIP: We used leftover Piano Key Borders from the Flower Garden quilt (pages 14 - 15) to make the stripes in this quilt.

We purchased *Moda* 'Ella' by Sentimental Studios collection of fabrics.

Piano Key Stripes:
  Purchase 1 strip 2½" x 21" of each fabric 1 - 25 from the Flower Garden Quilt on pages 14 - 15

Black Stripes and Black Border:
  Purchase 1½ yd of Black marbled

Border and Binding:
  Purchase 1¼ yd of Floral print

Backing
  Purchase 1½ yd, piece it to 48" x 68"

Batting
  Purchase 48" x 68"

Cutting

Stripes:
  Cut 1 strip 2½" x 21" of each color of fabrics 1 thru 25 (see colors on page 14)
  Cut 2 Black Stripes: 6½" x 50½"

Assemble Strips

Sew strips 1 thru 25 together in sequence (or use a leftover stripe from the Flower Garden Quilt). Press.

Cut the 25-strip set into 3 strips, each 6½" wide.

				25
				24
				23
				22
				21
				20
				19
				18
				17
				16
				15
				14
				13
				12
				11
				10
				9
				8
				7
				6
				5
				4
				3
				2
				1

Assemble Quilt Center
See Quilt Diagram

Sew the Center:
Sew a 25-strip set,
a Black 6½" x 50½" strip,
a 25-strip set,
a Black 6½" x 50½" strip,
and another 25-strip set together in rows.
Press.

continued from pages 46 - 49

Stack Bird Applique patterns in columns using patterns from pages 48 - 49 and 50 - 51.

Borders

Black Inner Border:
Cut 2 Black strips 1½" x 50½" for the sides.
Cut 2 Black strips 1½" x 32½" for the top and bottom.

Sew strips to the sides of the quilt. Press.
Sew strips to the top and bottom. Press.

Floral Outer Border:
Cut 2 Floral strips 6½" x 32½" for the top and bottom.
Cut 2 Floral strips 6½" x 64½" for the sides.

Sew the top and bottom borders to the quilt. Press.
Sew the side borders. Press.

Finishing

Applique:
See Basic Instructions on pages 58 - 61.
Embroidery:
Embroider bird feet, bird eyes, and butterfly antennae. See page 61.
Quilting: See Basic Instructions on pages 60.
Binding: See Basic Instructions on page 60.
Cut 6 strips 2½" x 40" and sew end to end for 220" of binding.

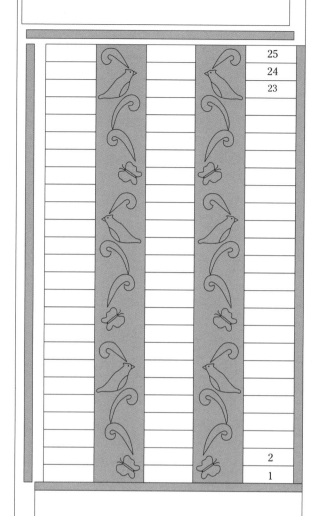

Quilt Assembly Diagram

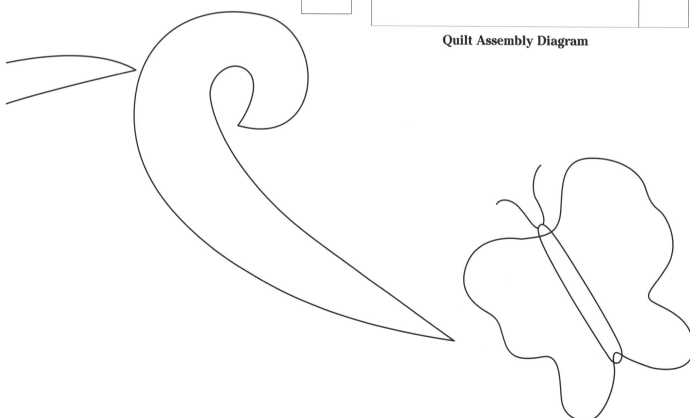

Folk Art Birds Quilt

continued from page 17

SIZE: 47" x 47"

Yardage

TIP: We used leftover Piano Key Borders from the Flower Garden quilt
(pages 14 - 15) to make the stripes in this quilt.

We purchased *Moda* 'Ella' by Sentimental Studios collection of fabrics

Inner Border	¼ yd each of fabrics 8 thru 23 (1 strip of each 2½" x 15") See the color swatches on page 14.
Black Blocks and Corners	Purchase 1 yd of Black Marbled
Outer Border and Binding	Purchase 1½ yd of Floral print
Appliques	Purchase ¼ yd each of Dark Red, Golden, Yellow, Medium Green Purchase 1¼ yd of Steam A Seam II fusible web
Backing	Purchase 1⅔ yd, piece it to 51" x 51"
Batting	Purchase 51" x 51"

Sewing machine, needle, thread

Cutting

Center Blocks:
Cut 4 Black squares 16½" x 16½".

Pieced Sashing:
Cut 1 strip each 2½" x 15" of fabrics 8 thru 23.
See Fabric swatches on page 14.

Corner Squares:
Cut 9 Black squares 2½" x 2½"

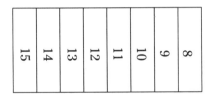

Prints to Yellows

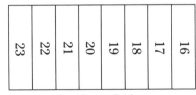

Purples to Reds

Assemble Strips

Sew 2½" x 15" strips 8 thru 15 together in sequence. Press.
Sew 2½" x 15" strips 16 thru 23 together in sequence. Press.

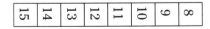

Prints to Yellows
Cut 6 strips, each 2½" x 16½"

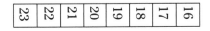

Purples to Reds
Cut 6 strips, each 2½" x 16½"

Cut 8-strip set sequences into 6 strips 2½" x 16½" each.

Assembly

See Quilt Diagram. Note the position of colors.

Row 1 - the Top Row:
Sew the Top Row:
An 8 thru 15 strip,
a 16½" x 16½" Black square,
an 8 thru 15 strip,
a 16½" x 16½" Black square,
an 8 thru 15 strip.
Press.

Row 2 - the Bottom Row:
Sew the Bottom Row:
A 16 thru 23 strip,
a 16½" x 16½" Black square,
a 16 thru 23,
a 16½" x 16½" Black square,
a 16 thru 23.
Press.

Horizontal Sashing Rows:

Make 3 Sashing Rows:
Sew a 2½" Black corner square,
a 23 thru 16 strip,
a 2½" Black corner square,
a 15 thru 8 strip,
a 2½" Black corner square.
Press.

Sew Rows Together:
a Horizontal Sashing Row,
Row 1 - the Top Row,
a Horizontal Sashing Row,
Row 2 - the Bottom Row,
a Horizontal Sashing Row,
Press.

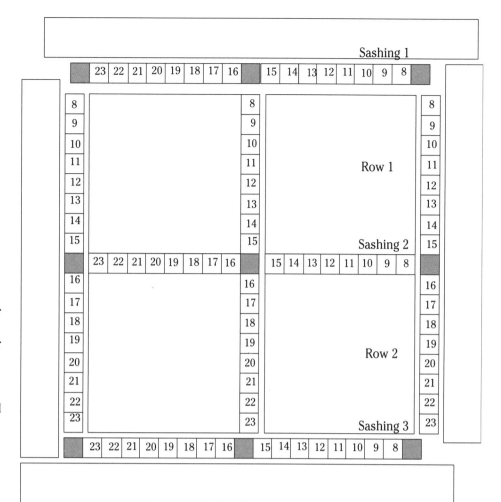

Borders

Floral Border:

Cut 2 strips 5" x 38½" for the sides.

Cut 2 strips 5" x 47½" for the top and bottom.

Sew strips to the sides. Press.

Sew strips to the top and bottom. Press.

Finishing

Applique:
See Basic Instructions on page 58.

Quilting:
See Basic Instructions on page 60.

Binding:
See Basic Instructions on page 60.
Cut 5 strips 2½" x 40" and sew end to end for 192" of binding.

Folk Art Birds Quilt Assembly

continued on pages 54 - 57

continued from pages 52 - 53

Folk Art Birds - Block 1

fold

Folk Art Birds - Block 2

fold

continued on pages 56 - 57

continued from pages 52 - 55

Folk Art Birds - Block 3

fold

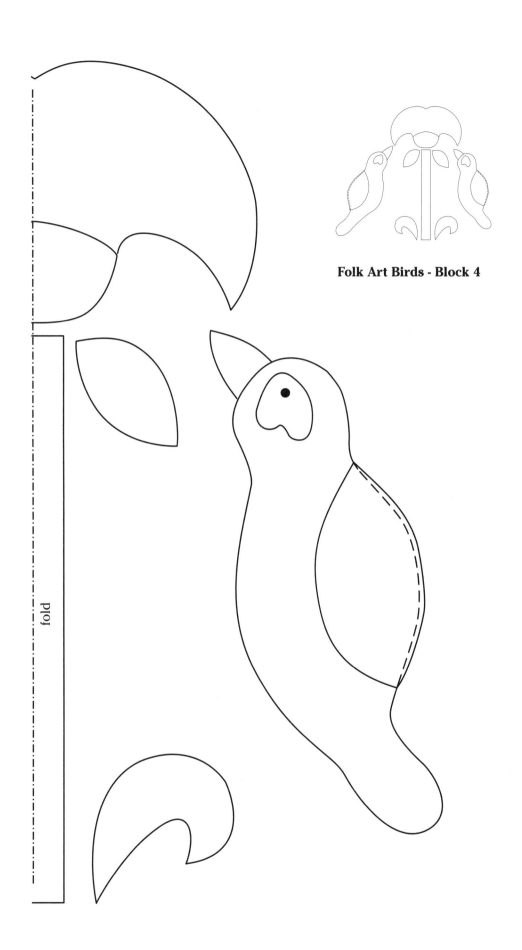

Folk Art Birds - Block 4

fold

Rotary Cutting Tips

Rotary Cutter: Friend or Foe

A rotary cutter is a wonderful and useful tool. When not used correctly, the sharp blade can be dangerous. Follow these safety tips:

1. Never cut toward you.

2. Use a sharp blade. Pressing harder on a dull blade can cause the blade to jump the ruler and injure your fingers.

3. Always disengage the blade before the cutter leaves your hand, even if you intend to pick it up immediately.

Rotary cutters have been caught when lifting fabric, have fallen onto the floor and have cut fingers.

Basic Cutting Instructions

Tips for Accurate Cutting:

Accurate cutting is easy when using a rotary cutter with a sharp blade, a cutting mat, and a transparent ruler. Begin by pressing your fabric and then follow these steps:

1. Folding:

a) Fold the fabric with the selvage edges together. Smooth the fabric flat. If needed, fold again to make your fabric length smaller than the length of the ruler.

b) Align the fold with one of the guide lines on the mat. This is important to avoid getting a kink in your strip.

2. Cutting:

a) Align the ruler with a guide line on the mat. Press down on the ruler to prevent it shifting or have someone help hold the ruler. Hold the rotary cutter along the edge of the ruler and cut off the selvage edge.

b) Also using the guide line on the mat, cut the ends straight.

c) Strips for the quilt top may be cut on the crosswise grain (from selvage to selvage) or on grain (parallel to the selvage edge).

If possible, cut strips for borders on grain (parallel to the selvage edge) to prevent wavy edges and make quilting easier.

d) When cutting strips, move the ruler, NOT the fabric.

Tips for Working with Strips

TIPS: As a Guide for Yardage:
Each ¼ yard or a 'Fat Quarter' equals 3 strips
A pre-cut 'Jelly Roll' strip is 2½" x 42"
Cut 'Fat Quarter' strips to 2½" x 21"

Pre-cut strips are cut on the crosswise grain and are prone to stretching. These tips will help reduce stretching and make your quilt lay flat for quilting.

1. If you are cutting yardage, cut on the grain. Whenever possible, cut fat quarters on grain, parallel to the 18" side.

2. When sewing crosswise grain strips together, take care not to stretch the strips. If you detect any puckering as you go, rip out the seam and sew it again.

3. Press, Do Not Iron. Carefully open fabric, with the seam to one side, press without moving the iron. A back-and-forth ironing motion stretches the fabric.

4. Reduce the wiggle in your borders with this technique from garment making. First, accurately cut your borders to the exact measure of the quilt top. Then, before sewing the border to the quilt, run a double row of stay stitches along the outside edge to maintain the original shape and prevent stretching. Pin the border to the quilt, taking care not to stretch the quilt top to make it fit. Pinning reduces slipping and stretching.

Basic Iron-On Applique Instructions

Using Fusible Web:

1. Trace the pattern onto fusible web and cut out.

2. Press the patterns onto the wrong side of the fabric.

3. Cut out patterns exactly on the drawn line.

4. Score the web paper with a pin to remove the paper.

5. Position the fabric, fusible side down, on the quilt and press with a hot iron following the fusible web manufacturer's instructions. Different brands require different heating times.

6. Stabilize the wrong side of the fabric with your favorite stabilizer.

7. Use a size 80 machine embroidery needle. Fill the bobbin with lightweight basting thread and thread the machine with a machine embroidery thread that complements the color being appliqued.

8. Set your machine for a Zigzag stitch and adjust the thread tension if needed. Use a scrap to experiment with different stitch widths and lengths until you find the one you like best.

9. Sew slowly.

| 1. Trace pattern onto fusible web and cut out. | 2. Press fusible web to the back of the fabric. | 3. Press fabrics onto the quilt top. |

Basic Turned Edge Applique Instructions

Using Freezer Paper:

1. Trace pattern onto freezer paper.

2. Press the waxy side of the freezer paper onto the wrong side of the fabric.

3. When you cut out the shape. leave a ⅛" fabric border all around. This will be turned under for a smooth edge.

4. Remove the freezer paper and turn it over so the waxy side is up.

5. Position the paper on the wrong side of the fabric and press the ⅛" border to the waxy paper with the tip of a hot iron. Press firmly.

6. Remove the paper if desired, maintaining the folded edge on the back of the fabric.

7. Position the shape on the quilt. Pin in position then Blindstitch in place.

Basic Sewing Instructions

You now have precisely cut strips that are exactly the correct width. You are well on your way to blocks that fit together perfectly. Accurate sewing is the next important step.

Matching Edges:

1. Carefully line up the edges of your strips. Many times, if the underside is off a little, your seam will be off by ⅛". This does not sound like much until you have 8 seams in a block, each off by ⅛". Now your finished block is a whole inch wrong!

2. Pin the pieces together to prevent them shifting.

Seam Allowance:

I cannot stress enough the importance of accurate ¼" seams. All the quilts in this book are measured for ¼" seams unless otherwise indicated.

Most sewing machine manufacturers offer a Quarter-inch foot. A Quarter-inch foot is the most worthwhile investment you can make in your quilting.

Pressing:

I want to talk about pressing even before we get to sewing because proper pressing can make the difference between a quilt that wins a ribbon at the quilt show and one that does not.

Press, do NOT iron. What does that mean? Many of us want to move the iron back and forth along the seam. This "ironing" stretches the strip out of shape and creates errors that accumulate as the quilt is constructed. Believe it or not, there is a correct way to press your seams, and here it is:

1. Do NOT use steam with your iron. If you need a little water, spritz it on.

2. Place your fabric flat on the ironing board without opening the seam. Set a hot iron on the seam and count to 3. Lift the iron and move to the next position along the seam. Repeat until the entire seam is pressed. This sets and sinks the threads into the fabric.

3. Now, carefully lift the top strip and fold it away from you so the seam is on one side. Usually the seam is pressed toward the darker fabric, but often the direction of the seam is determined by the piecing requirements.

4. Press the seam open with your fingers. Add a little water or spray starch if it wants to close again. Lift the iron and place it on the seam. Count to 3. Lift the iron again and continue until the seam is pressed. Do NOT use the tip of the iron to push the seam open. So many people do this and wonder later why their blocks are not fitting together.

5. Most critical of all: For accuracy every seam must be pressed before the next seam is sewn.

Working with Crosswise Grain strips:

Strips cut on the crosswise grain (from selvage to selvage) have problems similar to bias edges and are prone to stretching. To reduce stretching and make your quilt lay flat for quilting, keep these tips in mind.

1. Take care not to stretch the strips as you sew.

2. Adjust the sewing thread tension and the presser foot pressure if needed.

3. If you detect any puckering as you go, rip out the seam and sew it again. It is much easier to take out a seam now than to do it after the block is sewn.

Sewing Bias Edges:

Bias edges wiggle and stretch out of shape very easily. They are not recommended for beginners, but even a novice can accomplish bias edges if these techniques are employed.

1. Stabilize the bias edge with one of these methods:

a) Press with spray starch.

b) Press freezer paper or removable iron-on stabilizer to the back of the fabric.

c) Sew a double row of stay stitches along the bias edge and ⅛" from the bias edge. This is a favorite technique of garment makers.

2. Pin, pin, pin! I know pinning takes extra time, but when working with bias edges, pinning makes the difference between items that match and those that do not.

Building Better Borders:

Wiggly borders make a quilt very difficult to finish. However, wiggly borders can be avoided with these techniques.

1. Cut the borders on grain. That means cutting your strips parallel to the selvage edge.

2. Accurately cut your borders to the exact measure of the quilt.

3. If your borders are piece stripped from crosswise grain fabrics, press well with spray starch and sew a double row of stay stitches along the outside edge to maintain the original shape and prevent stretching.

4. Pin the border to the quilt, taking care not to stretch the quilt top to make it fit. Pinning reduces slipping and stretching.

Basic Layering Instructions

Marking Your Quilt:

If you choose to mark your quilt for hand or machine quilting, it is much easier to do so before layering. Press your quilt before you begin. Here are some handy tips regarding marking.

1. A disappearing pen may vanish before you finish.

2. Use a White pencil on dark fabrics.

3. If using a washable Blue pen, remember that pressing may make the pen permanent.

Pieced Backings:

1. Press the backing fabric before measuring.

2. If possible cut backing fabrics on grain, parallel to the selvage edges.

3. Piece 3 parts rather than 2 whenever possible, sewing 2 side borders to the center. This reduces stress on the pieced seam.

4. The backing and batting should extend at least 2" on each side of the quilt.

Creating a Quilt Sandwich:

1. Press the backing and top to remove all wrinkles.

2. Lay the backing wrong side up on the table.

3. Position the batting over the backing and smooth out all wrinkles.

4. Center the quilt top over the batting leaving a 2" border all around.

5. Pin the layers together with 2" safety pins positioned a handwidth apart. A grapefruit spoon makes inserting the pins easier. Leaving the pins open in the container speeds up the basting on the next quilt.

Basic Quilting Instructions

Hand Quilting:

Many quilters enjoy the serenity of hand quilting. Because the quilt is handled a great deal, it is important to securely baste the sandwich together. Place the quilt in a hoop and don't forget to hide your knots.

Machine Quilting:

All quilts in this book were machine quilted. Some were quilted on a large, free-arm quilting machine and others were quilted on a sewing machine. If you have never machine quilted before, practice on scraps first.

Straight Line Machine Quilting Tips:

1. Pin baste the layers securely.

2. Set up your sewing machine with a size 80 quilting needle and a walking foot.

3. Experimenting with decorative stitches on your machine adds interest to your quilt. You do not have to quilt the entire piece with the same stitch. Variety is the spice of life, so have fun trying out new stitches as well as your favorite stand-bys.

Free Motion Machine Quilting Tips:

1. Pin baste the layers securely.

2. Set up your sewing machine with a spring needle, a quilting foot, and lower the feed dogs.

Basic Binding Instructions

A Perfect Finish:

The binding endures the most stress on a quilt and is usually the first thing to wear out. For this reason, we recommend using a double fold binding.

1. Trim the backing and batting even with the quilt edge.

2. If possible cut strips on the crosswise grain because a little bias in the binding is a Good thing. This is the only place in the quilt where bias is helpful, for it allows the binding to give as it is turned to the back and sewn in place.

3. Strips are usually cut 2½" wide, but check the instructions for your project before cutting.

4. Sew strips end to end to make a long strip sufficient to go all around the quilt plus 4"- 6".

5. With wrong sides together, fold strip in half lengthwise. Press.

6. Stretch out your hand and place your little finger at the corner of the quilt top. Place the binding where your thumb touches the edge of the quilt. Aligning the edge of the quilt with the raw edges of the binding, pin the binding in place along the first side.

7. Leaving a 2" tail for later use, begin sewing the binding to the quilt with a ¼" seam.

For Mitered Corners:

1. Stop ¼" from the first corner. Leave the needle in the quilt and turn it 90°. Hit the reverse button on your machine and back off the quilt leaving the threads connected.

2. Fold the binding perpendicular to the side you sewed, making a 45° angle. Carefully maintaining the first fold, bring the binding back along the edge to be sewn.

3. Carefully align the edges of the binding with quilt edge and sew as you did the first side. Repeat this process until you reach the tail left at the beginning. Fold the tail out of the way, sew until you are ¼" from the beginning stitches.

4. Remove the quilt from the machine. Fold quilt out of the way and match the binding tails together. Carefully sew the binding tails with a ¼" seam. Do this by hand if you prefer.

Finishing the Binding:

5. Trim the seam to reduce bulk.

6. Finish stitching the binding to the quilt across the join you just sewed.

7. Turn the binding to the back of the quilt. To reduce bulk at the corners, fold the miter in the opposite direction from which it was folded on the front.

8. Hand-sew a Blind stitch on the back of the quilt to secure the binding in place.

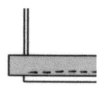 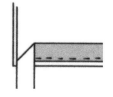

Align raw edge of the binding with the raw edge of quilt top. Start about 8" from the corner, go along the first side with a ¼" seam.	Stop ¼" from the edge. Stitch a slant to the corner (through both layers of binding)... lift up, then down, as you line up the edge. Fold the binding back.	Align raw edge again. Continue stitching the next side with a ¼" seam as you sew binding in place.

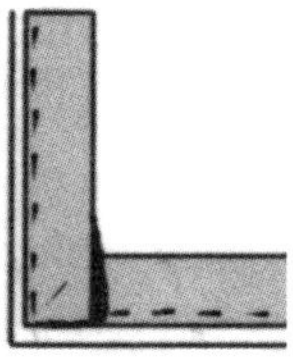

Basic Embroidery Stitches

Little hand embroidered touches such as eyes and feet on birds, flower stamens, and leaf veins are beautifully accomplished with simple Straight stitches and French Knots.

Use 2 strands of embroidery floss for thin lines and small eyes. Use 3 strands for thicker lines and outside edges.

Straight Stitch

Come up at A and go down at B to form a simple flat stitch. Use this stitch for hair for animals and for simple petals on small flowers.

Running Stitch

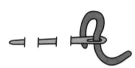

Come up at A. Weave the needle through the fabric, making short, even stitches. Use this stitch to gather fabrics, too.

Stem Stitch

Work from left to right to make regular, slanting stitches along the stitch line. Bring the needle up above the center of the last stitch. Also called 'Outline' stitch.

French Knot

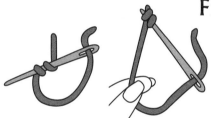

Come up at A. Wrap the floss around the needle 2 to 3 times. Insert the needle close to A. Hold the floss and pull the needle through the loops gently.

Lazy Daisy Stitch

Come up at A. Go down at B (right next to A) to form a loop. Come back up at C with the needle tip over the thread. Go down at D to make a small anchor stitch over the top of the loop.

Whip Stitch

Insert the needle under a few fibers of one layer of fabric. Bring the needle up through the other layer of fabric. Use this stitch to attach the folded raw edges of fabric to the back of pieces or to attach bindings around the edges of quilts and coverlets.

Blanket Stitch

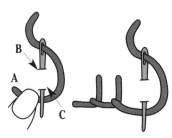

Come up at A, hold the thread down with your thumb, go down at B. Come back up at C with the needle tip over the thread. Pull the stitch into place. Repeat, outlining with the bottom legs of the stitch. Use this stitch to edge fabrics.

Design Tips with 'Jelly Rolls'

I love quilting with 'Jelly Roll' collections of 2½" pre-cut fabric strips. With 'Jelly Rolls' it is possible to complete a quilt top in a weekend.

I want to share a few tips for working with 'Jelly Rolls'. The colors are always beautiful together and create the handmade scrappy look that is so popular today.

My first step in designing is to divide the strips into groups of color... Greens, Purples, Browns, Tans, etc. Next I estimate the number of strips I will need for the blocks.

Sometimes I need an extra strip or two of a color, let's say Green so I look for a Tan with a lot of Green print and move it to the Green stack.... and the same with any other color.

Enjoy quilting...

Suzanne McNeill

Place Mats

see photo on page 67

Note: We used leftovers from a *Moda* 'Folklorique' by Fig Tree 'Jelly Roll' collection of pre-cut 2½" fabric strips.

SIZE: 12" x 18"

Yardage for Red Rose Mat

Place Mat:
  6 Cream strips 2½" x 18½" (½ yd)

Applique: 2 Red strips 2½" x 21"
           1 Green strip 2½" x 21"

Backing: 12½" x 18½"

Binding: 4 Green strips 2½" x 21"

Batting: 12½" x 18½" rectangle

Assembly

Place Mat Top: Sew 6 Cream strips together side by side to make a 12½" x 18½" rectangle. Press.

Rose Applique:

Sew 2 Red strips together side by side. Trace the rose design and cut from the Red strips.

Trace the stem and leaf designs and cut from the Green strip. See Basic Instructions for Fusible Applique on page 58.

Layer backing and place mat with wrong sides together. Sew all around the outer edge with a scant ¼" seam.

Finishing

Quilting:
See Basic Instructions on pages 58 - 61.

Binding:
See Basic Instructions on page 60.
Sew 2½" x 21" strips end to make 80".

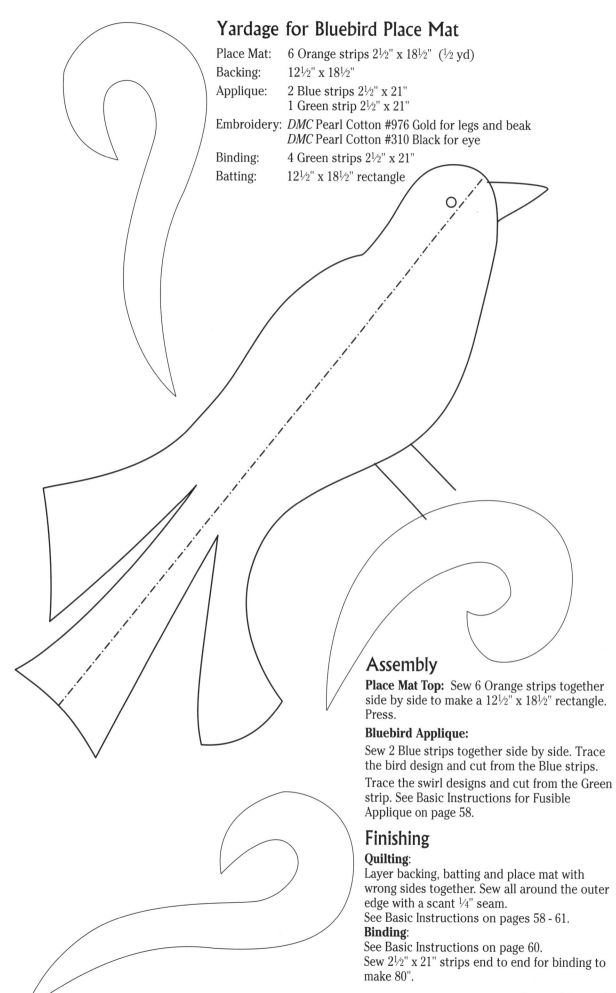

Yardage for Bluebird Place Mat

Place Mat: 6 Orange strips 2½" x 18½" (½ yd)

Backing: 12½" x 18½"

Applique: 2 Blue strips 2½" x 21"
1 Green strip 2½" x 21"

Embroidery: *DMC* Pearl Cotton #976 Gold for legs and beak
DMC Pearl Cotton #310 Black for eye

Binding: 4 Green strips 2½" x 21"

Batting: 12½" x 18½" rectangle

Assembly

Place Mat Top: Sew 6 Orange strips together side by side to make a 12½" x 18½" rectangle. Press.

Bluebird Applique:

Sew 2 Blue strips together side by side. Trace the bird design and cut from the Blue strips.

Trace the swirl designs and cut from the Green strip. See Basic Instructions for Fusible Applique on page 58.

Finishing

Quilting:

Layer backing, batting and place mat with wrong sides together. Sew all around the outer edge with a scant ¼" seam.

See Basic Instructions on pages 58 - 61.

Binding:

See Basic Instructions on page 60.

Sew 2½" x 21" strips end to end for binding to make 80".

Hot Pads

see photo on page 67

SIZE: 8" x 8"

Yardage for 3 Posies Hot Pad

Note: We used leftovers from a *Moda* 'Folklorique' by Fig Tree 'Jelly Roll' collection of pre-cut 2½" fabric strips.

Hot Pad:	4 strips Orange 2½" x 8½"
	4 strips Green 2½" x 8½"
Backing:	8½" x 8½" square
Appliques:	3 Red strips 2½" x 21"
	3 Blue strips 2½" x 21"
	1 Brown strip 2½" x 21"
Binding:	2 Cream strips 2½" x 21"
Batting:	8½" x 8½" square

Assembly

Hot Pad Top: Sew 4 Orange strips together side by side to make an 8½" x 8½" square. Sew 4 Green strips side by side to make an 8½" x 8½" square. Press.

Cut each square into two pieces. Cut diagonally ¼" from the center line. discard the smaller triangle or use it to make a smaller hot pad.

Sew a triangle of color A to a triangle of color B.

Posies Applique: Sew 3 Red strips together side by side. Sew 3 Blue strips together side by side. Trace the posy circles, stems and leaf design and cut designs from the strips. See Basic Instructions for Fusible Applique on page 58.

Finishing

Quilting: Layer backing, batting and hot pad with wrong sides together. Sew all around the outer edge with a scant ¼" seam. See Basic Instructions on pages 58 - 61.

Binding: See Basic Instructions on page 60.

Sew 2½" x 21" Cream strips end to end for binding.

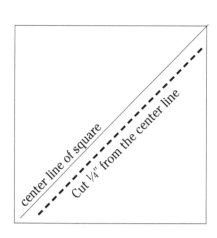

center line of square

Cut ¼" from the center line

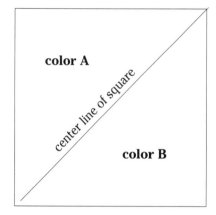

color A

center line of square

color B

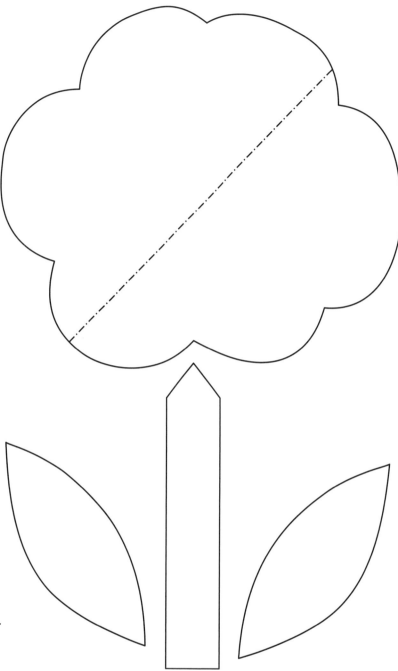

see photo on page 67

SIZE: 8" x 8"

Assembly

Hot Pad Top: Sew 4 Cream strips together side by side to make an 8½" x 8½" square. Sew 4 Green strips side by side to make an 8½" x 8½" square. Press.

Cut each square into two pieces. Cut diagonally ¼" from the center line. discard the smaller triangle or use it to make a smaller hot pad.

Sew a triangle of color A to a triangle of color B.

Rose Applique: Sew 3 Red strips together side by side. Trace the rose, stem and leaf designs and cut designs from the strips. See Basic Instructions for Fusible Applique on page 58.

Finishing

Quilting:
Layer backing, batting and hot pad with wrong sides together. Sew all around the outer edge with a scant ¼" seam.
See Basic Instructions on pages 58 - 61.
Binding:
See Basic Instructions on page 60.
Sew 2½" x 21" strips end to end for binding.

Yardage for Red Rose Hot Pad

Note: We used leftovers from a *Moda* 'Folklorique' by Fig Tree 'Jelly Roll' collection of pre-cut 2½" fabric strips.

Hot Pad:	4 strips Cream 2½" x 8½"
	4 strips Green 2½" x 8½"
Backing:	8½" x 8½" square
Appliques:	3 Red strips 2½" x 21"
	1Green strip 2½" x 21"
Binding:	2 Cream strips 2½" x 21"
Batting:	8½" x 8½" square

Place Mats
Bluebird and Red Rose
continued on pages 58 - 59
Decorate your table every day with beautiful handmade place mats. And the best part is that we made ours from leftover strips.

Hot Pads
Posies • Rose • Bluebird
continued on pages 61 - 62
With smaller leftovers, create colorful trivets and hot pads with whimsical applique birds and flowers.

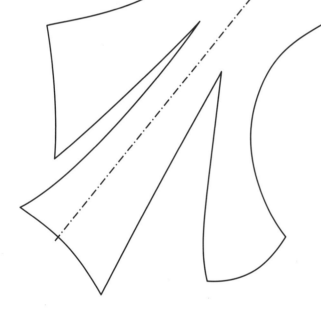

"Waste not - Want not."

SIZE: 8" x 8"

Yardage for Bluebird Hot Pad
Note: We used leftovers from a *Moda* 'Folklorique' by Fig Tree 'Jelly Roll' collection of pre-cut 2½" fabric strips.

Hot Pad: 4 Cream strips 2½" x 9"

Backing: 8½" x 8½" square

Applique: 2 Blue strips 2½" x 21"

Binding: 2 Blue strips 2½" x 21"

Batting: 8½" x 8½" square

Embroidery:
    DMC Pearl Cotton #976 Gold for legs and beak
    DMC Pearl Cotton #310 Black for eye

Assembly
Hot Pad Top: Sew 4 Cream strips side by side to make an 8½" x 8½" square. Press.

Bird Applique: Sew 2 Blue strips together side by side. Trace the bird design and cut bird from the strips. See Basic Instructions for Fusible Applique on page 58.

Add hand embroidered details for the eye, legs and beak. See page 61.

Finishing
Quilting: Layer backing, batting and hot pad with wrong sides together. Sew all around the outer edge with a scant ¼" seam. See Basic Instructions on pages 58 - 61.

Binding: See Basic Instructions on page 60.
    Sew 2½" x 21" Blue strips end to end for binding.

Supplier - Most craft and variety stores carry an excellent assortment of supplies. If you need something special, ask your local store to contact the following companies.

FABRICS, 'JELLY ROLLS', 'FAT QUARTERS'
   Moda and United Notions, Dallas, TX 1
QUILTERS
   Susan Corbett, 817-361-7762
   Julie Lawson, 817-428-5929
   Nanc Christopherson, 817-313-4959
   Donna Akins, 817-469-7102
STEAM A SEAM II FUSIBLE WEB
   the Warm Company
PEARL COTTON and FLOSS
   DMC